A BLACK GIRL IN THE MIDDLE

A Black Girl in the Middle

ESSAYS ON
(Allegedly)
FIGURING IT ALL OUT

Shenequa Golding

HEADLINE

First published in the United Kingdom 2024 by
HEADLINE PUBLISHING GROUP
First published in the US in 2024 by Beacon Press

1

Cataloguing in Publication Data is available from the British Library

Hardback ISBN: 978 1 4722 9770 9

Offset in 10.34/14.1pt Adobe Caslon Pro by Jouve (UK), Milton Keynes

Printed and bound in Great Britain by Clays Ltd, Elcograf S.p.A.

Headline's policy is to use papers that are natural, renewable and recyclable
products and made from wood grown in well-managed forests and other
controlled sources. The logging and manufacturing processes are expected to
conform to the environmental regulations of the country of origin.

HEADLINE PUBLISHING GROUP
An Hachette UK Company
Carmelite House
50 Victoria Embankment
London EC4Y 0DZ

www.headline.co.uk
www.hachette.co.uk

*This book is dedicated to everyone
who has ever called Oceania Street home.
Thank you.
(That includes you too, Dallas.)*

CONTENTS

Black Girl Math

"**H**i, my name's Shenequa and I'll be your server tonight. What will you be having to drink?"

"Two waters," the man said. "And can you please bring us the bread?"

The summer going into my senior year of college I waitressed at a local Italian restaurant. It was one of two jobs I had that year to help pay for Roxy (my Nissan Altima) and my off-campus apartment. Rushing to work from campus after my last class, I snuck in by the back door of the restaurant, frantically tying my apron around my waist with my notepad stuffed in my mouth.

"Golding!" my manager barked.

"Sorry," I replied sheepishly. "My professor is long-winded."

"Get in there," he said, handing me two menus. "A couple just got seated at table seventeen."

After returning with their waters, I placed the garlic bread in the middle of the table and drizzled seasoned olive oil onto a saucer for the couple to enjoy with their loaf. After they took a few bites, I bent down in front of the table and placed the notepad on my knee ready to take their order. The man saw my fatigue and inquired.

"I pulled a double shift the night before and this is my second job, so I'm beat," I explained.

"Ah man, what did you say your name was again?" he asked.

"Me? I'm Shenequa," I said as I wrote the woman's order.

"And you worked a double?" he said, ripping a piece of bread from the loaf. "So, how many kids do you have?"

I'm going to let that last sentence hang in the air for a bit and mention that this couple was indeed white.

I never got their names, but he looked like he could be a Ted and the woman, I assumed his wife, could be a Mary. Ted and Mary could've met in high school, or maybe they gained the courage to love each other after leaving their respective spouses now that the kids were out of the house. Who knows? I'm not sure if Maybe Ted assumed I was the mother of fifty-leven kids because of my name or because I'm a Black girl who worked all day. I can't say for certain that if my name were Ashley he would've come to his same racist conclusion. What I do know is that Maybe Ted forced me to do some quick Black girl math.

Often I have to decide just how much *Black girl* a moment of disrespect merits. There's Level One, which includes the ten-second-or-less death stare. It's quick, frosty, and meant to inform the offender they have caused offense. The energy in the room is now off.

Level Two is the lifted eyebrow or eye roll. (If said Black girl is anywhere from the Caribbean, the eye roll is replaced with sucking her teeth.)

Level Three might include a quick flick of the wrist, almost to shoo away a fly, when in actuality she's dismissing the comment to maintain professionalism. She might sprinkle in a "whatever" for added value.

Level Four might be sub-tweeting the offender in real life while the person is within earshot. For example: "*I know this white man did not just . . .*" The Black girl may chuckle or laugh, but nothing's really funny. If the offender doesn't respond, the moment can be brought back down to a Level Two. If the offender is brave enough to engage, then we're entering new territory.

Level Five is when the body language shifts. The Black girl may tilt her head to the side (most likely the right), look the offender up and down, and follow up with: "Is there a problem?" The tone is measured, and the question is rhetorical.

Level Six usually includes an expletive.

Level Seven is similar to Level Six in the way language is employed, however, instead of a ripe four-letter word, said Black girl might use the elongated "waiiiiiiiiit" or, in a pinch, "excusssssse me!" The length of the words adds a bit of drama, yes, but also allows everyone in the vicinity time to gather their belongings and vacate before something goes awry. The "waiiiiiiiiit" is a de facto warning.

Level Eight includes a hand gesture in the vicinity of the transgressor's face.

Level Nine invokes the language of Level Six, the hand gesture of Level Eight, but now she's adding forward movement to it, by walking in the direction of the offender.

And if you're still around for Level Ten, well, Godspeed. Level Ten is reserved for cheating boyfriends and white women who admire Susan B. Anthony and "don't see color."

Depending on how egregious the offense, say, for instance, a white man assuming you have multiple kids to feed because you're a Black girl named Shenequa, then that Black girl could've very likely exploded and forgotten the math. It should be noted that not all Black girls adhere to this particular formula. Some skip over the first six levels and immediately start at Level Seven. Others may combine the Level One death stare with the wrist action of Level Three. There are some Black girls who don't adhere to any of this math to protect their own sanity, and the Black girls in corporate settings have learned Black girl math will only lead to the "angry Black woman" stereotyping from bald-headed Bill in accounting. While HR and the new Diversity, Equity, and Inclusion officer might say they'll "investigate the matter," we all know the outcome may be less than favorable.

When you're a Black girl maneuvering through these moments, you must reduce your justified response by 60 percent because you're expected to handle any situation with the grace your transgressor was divorced from. If every Black girl reacted to every modicum of disrespect, then we'd never accomplish our goals. And so, most Black girls have learned to swallow their frustration and continue with the day.

It was Ted, excuse me, *Maybe* Ted's incessant chomping on bread that almost made me flip the entire table over. After leaving the safety and comfort of Hampton University's all-Black campus to then be confronted with this off-the-cuff racism was a shock to say the least. The fact that he still had an appetite after so bluntly making his comment upped my Black girl reaction to Level Nine, but remembering that I was a broke college student and he was a white man, I brought it down to a Level Three.

"I don't have any kids," I said with a tight jaw. "I'm in college and I'm working to purchase my textbooks."

Maybe Ted's cheeks shone red like a tomato. He nodded, aware of the comment he made, but never apologized. He looked at Could Be Mary, as if ignoring me would make me disappear faster. She remained on brand with her vacant "What day is it, again?" stare, as if that was going to help the situation. They both looked frightened, like I might call NAACP headquarters and report them for being bad whites, because not only are all Black girls named Shenequa working to support nineteen of their children, but we also have the NAACP phone number memorized. And if no one from the office picks up, we snap our fingers and poof! Al Sharpton or Ben Crump magically appears.

It's been more than fifteen years since that encounter, but I'll never forget Maybe Ted's face and the confidence he spoke with when he learned my name. Oddly enough, that was the first and last time any white person has ever publicly commented on my name in a negative fashion. Every other criticism I've received has come from my own people, folks who look like me, may have had similar experiences as me, but still felt justified in assuming the worst about me based on my name.

. . .

A few years back, I left a business meeting in Harlem and took the train downtown to Penn Station. I stopped inside of a Starbucks and ordered one of their cold, fruity drinks. At the time, I didn't speak fluent Starbucks, so I would rehearse my order while waiting in line to make it sound hip and edgy like all the other grande-mocha-frappe-two-pumps-skim-milk-no-whip folks. Yet despite my preparation, I'd get to the barista, stutter and sweat from the pressure because of the line behind me and the one asshat who sighed loud as hell. Crumbling from being so overwhelmed, I'd usually ask for a small fruity shaboing.

What's a "shaboing"?

Right, valid question. A "shaboing" is my personal catchall word. If someone gives me directions, I say *shaboing* to confirm receipt. If I'm at the gym, out of breath, and I point to the ten-pound kettlebell, I'll say: "Hey, can you please pass me that shaboing?" Or, in this instance, Starbucks' newest cold, fruity drink is also called a medium mango–passion fruit shaboing.

After ordering, the barista, a person of color, asked for my name.

"S-H-E-N-E-Q-U-A," I spelled.

"Shenequa?" he questioned. "Wow. I wouldn't peg you for a Shenequa."

I took a deep, Mississippi Delta wade in the water, *I might not get to the promised land with you*, sigh. I knew I should've left it alone. I should've just asked for my change, waited for my grande shaboing, and gone about my business, but curiosity got the best of me. I could already tell that whatever he would say next wasn't going to be good, but I went against my better judgment and asked anyway.

"Really? Why do you say that?"

"Well, you're not straight-up dark-skinned," he said, using his hip to close the register while handing me my change. "You look like an Abby or something. Following guest!"

Silence.

This comment caught me so off guard I couldn't even do the math to determine what level of Black girl this barista deserved. Instead, I just became constipated, which is a useless reaction to someone's foolish colorist beliefs, but there I was inside a Penn Station Starbucks backed up like somebody's iCloud.

"Ma'am," the barista said. "Excuse me, ma'am. Your drink will be ready for you at the end of the counter. There's a line."

The barista insulted me and then dismissed me in one swift motion. His slight was impressive as far as multilayered offenses are concerned. Due to my lighter skin tone, I allegedly deserve a more *dignified*, mainstream name like Abby—a name that's closer to the proximity of whiteness he envisioned for me. Not one where my Blackness has made a home in, the Blackness supposedly only designated for dark-skinned girls, the Blackness he felt so comfortable disrespecting. From our brief encounter, the barista deduced I wasn't Black enough for my Black-ass name.

And whether he knew it or not or read books about the topic or not, the barista's "you're not straight-up dark-skinned" comment was disrespectful. I should've, like elders sometimes say, "just followed my first mind" and went about my day.

. . .

The name Shenequa has weight. It's eight letters that require your lips and tongue to work. It comes equipped with the letters *q* and *u* and doesn't beget the "simplicity" of Emily, Ashley, or Sarah. There isn't a generally accepted abbreviation for Shenequa, like Bill is for William. Shenequa requires thought and purpose. Shenequa, with all its black pepper and smoked paprika, requires intention. I wish I could say my mother had some grand plan when she named me, but she didn't. I would love to say that when she had me at sixteen years old, my mother had enough vision to know I'd turn this name and the stereotype associated with it on its head to show a Shenequa could be just as elegant and as thoughtful as a Megan or Jill is perceived to be. Unfortunately, that wasn't the case. Once Mommy learned she was having a girl she zeroed in on the name Adrien. There was a woman named Adrien Arpel who had a skincare line she liked, so Mommy decided she would name me after the random skincare lady.

But somewhere between me being born and Mommy signing the birth certificate, a family friend suggested the name Shenequa. Mommy liked it. She thought it was different and so that's what she went with—Shenequa Adrien Golding. I didn't know my name was an "issue" until I got older. I was raised around a diverse crop of kids all throughout school and even college. I went to school with kids who were named after days of the week, seasons, and foods the Greek gods allegedly ate, so for me my name was just my name. I later learned in life that when some people think of a Shenequa, they think ghetto, loud, and assume that Shenequa has multiple baby daddies or uses her bedazzled manicured pinky nail as an additional fork to retrieve food stuck in the back of her tooth at a dinner table. "Ghetto" Black women, especially named Shenequa, in some people's minds are a threat to society.

In the early 2000s, Little-T and One Track Mike created the insanely sticky "Shaniqua (Don't Live Here No More)," a song about a college student (Little T) who receives count-less phone calls to his dorm room from strangers looking for the popular yet mysterious Shaniqua. The hook: "Shaniqua don't live here no more"[1] became people's way of familiarizing themselves with me upon introduction. They'd know nothing about me or my musical taste, but they knew that song, so that was where they chose to meet me. It wasn't: "I also love traveling" or "*Babysitter Club Books* were my fave growing up too!" It was usually: "Hey, do you remember that song from back in the day? It used to be on *TRL*? It goes 'Shaniqua don't live . . .'"

And if Little-T and One Track Mike didn't help with the borderline graceless branding of my name, *Martin*'s Sheneneh Jenkins locked it in. Played by Martin Lawrence during his '90s sitcom, Sheneneh lived across the hall and never missed an opportunity to be in everyone's business. She was loud, rude, and brazen. Her attire was excessive and her costume jewelry gaudy. You also couldn't tell her she wasn't cute. Sheneneh was a fan favorite because she was funny, and her comebacks were slick and sharp. Even I remember laughing *with* her when she appeared on the screen because despite how she behaved, Sheneneh owned the scene whenever she was in it.

But her over-the-top personality, along with the similarity in our names, was an assumption placed on me I had to divorce myself from if I wanted to be taken seriously when meeting new people. Sheneneh was a joke and I had to quickly establish that I was not. Martin, however, wasn't the only one earning LOLs at a Black woman's expense. On *In Living Color*, Jamie Foxx brought Wanda Wayne to life, a platinum wig–wearing Black woman who could "rock your world." Her (Jamie's) protruding lips, made more prominent by her poorly applied red lipstick, was yet another example of Black women being made into a mockery. Jim Carrey played Vera de Milo, a "female" bodybuilder with a flat chest, deep voice, a huge bulge, and pigtails. So yes, Keenan Ivory Wayans was an equal opportunity offender, but when white men make fun of other white people, it's never an indictment on them or their entire community. Black men in the 1990s and early 2000s dressed as exaggerated versions of Black women meant they earned a pat on the back from an audience and a paycheck. Black women were the ones who had to duck and dodge the real stigma that came along with it. As a teen and young twentysomething-year-old, I had to laugh along with the Sheneneh jokes, or the "Shaniqua don't live here no more" quips. To show any of my annoyance would've "killed the vibe" and if I was already fighting off the Sheneneh comparison, I damn sure didn't have the bandwidth left to deal with the "Someone's being sensitive" rebuttal that would've come had I employed a more assertive approach. When you're a Black girl, it can often feel like you're damned if you do and you're damned if you don't.

. . .

My name, and the stereotype that comes with it, gets a bad rap, but compared to a slew of celebrity children, Shenequa is the iOS updated version of Barbara.

Kim Kardashian and Kanye West named their eldest child a direction (North), their middle kid a holy person (Saint), their second baby girl a city (Chicago), and their youngest a book from the Bible (Psalm). Travis Scott and Kylie Jenner picked Stormi (with an i) for their daughter. Cardi B and Offset's cutie-patootie children (who look just alike) are named Kulture and Wave. Maroon 5 front man Adam Levine and his wife chose Dusty Rose as a name for their kid. And Gwyneth Paltrow and Chris Martin thought Apple was a suitable name for their first born. Listen, I'm here for all these names, because why not? They're unique, and intentional. However, the name that brings me the most pleasure comes from Oscar-winner Kate Winslet, who named her son Bear Blaze.

Speaking with Ellen DeGeneres some years back, Winslet said she met her husband while staying at billionaire Richard Branson's home on his private island, when the house caught fire. No one was hurt, but to commemorate their fiery first meeting, the couple decided their son's middle name should be Blaze, which I'm fine with because I grew up listening to Just Blaze. As far as how the boy earned his first name, Bear, Kate said a childhood friend had the nickname and she's always loved it. So, Kate Winslet can name her son Bear Blaze, yet a Black girl from Queens named Shenequa obviously has thirty-four kids to support. Will Bear Blaze catch some flak for his name? Maybe, but will that stop people from assuming he can't carry out the job? Probably not.

In 2015, Raven-Symoné, who was then a co-host on the daytime talk show *The View*, boldly said she wouldn't employ anyone with "a ghetto" name. "I'm not going to hire you if your name is Watermelondrea. That's just not going to happen. I'm not going to hire you," she said proudly.[2]

At this point in her life, Ms. Symoné had already made her politics surrounding Blackness known, but her comment was triggering nonetheless. Some might read this and say "Well, only hit dogs holler. Raven-Symoné's opinion would only upset a girl named Shenequa if she thought her name was ghetto." My response would be "Why is anyone hitting dogs to begin with?" Has PETA not petitioned to get this old adage eradicated? You know why Raven-Symoné's "Watermelondrea" comment hurt? It's because the name was exaggerated and it felt deliberately disrespectful. I think a lot of people believe most Black American names are simply fictitious, and thus shouldn't be respected. In front of an audience full of people and countless others watching at home, Raven-Symoné gave folks permission to throw my resume, my college degree, my accomplishments, my humor, my work ethic, and my humanity into the trash bin because of my name. And how do we not know Watermelondrea doesn't mean wise, compassionate, brave, or kind? Her comment was so insensitive and hurt more because this lack of compassion came from a Black woman.

My name doesn't bother me; it's the fact that so many people prejudge me before meeting me *because* of my name that hurts. Raven-Symoné's employment assessment was also coming from a woman named after a bird.

Pot, please meet my friend, kettle.

Jokes aside, names have meanings, but they also bear a perceived context. Raven-Symoné's name is beautiful. A quick Google search will show the name Raven means dark-haired and wise and Symoné means listener. I dug into my name and everything from "a tree planted by water," "marvelous," to "a child of God" popped up. If the meanings behind names were more wildly known and accepted, than the assumed character and personality of a person donning a name, this world would be a little less judgmental and I would need a new opening chapter.

To avoid the "Shenequa effect," some Black parents neutralize their children's name, maybe hoping this can advance them later in life. Singer-songwriter and actress Jill Scott revealed on her podcast that her full name is actually Jill Heather Scott! A Black girl from North Philly who's experienced hard times like the rest of us was given a name that some, like the Penn Station Starbucks barista, wouldn't attribute to a North Philly girl. Jill. Heather. Scott! The exclamation mark wasn't to add crescendo to the sentence or a typo; it's because Scott also revealed that her mother, Ms. Joyce Scott, gave her Black daughter this name and intentionally added the exclamation point because, why not? So, there you have it. Jill Heather Scott! has an exclamation mark on her birth certificate, and my name is Shenequa, and the world didn't explode.

There have been times after introducing myself to men that I've been accused of lying. I've heard: "Yo, you look too good to be named Shenequa," because obviously all Shenequas are raging swamp donkeys that look like the before picture in any acne commercial. Or my personal favorite: "C'mon shorty, don't stand there and front like your name is *really* Shenequa, like . . ." You're right. I was lying. My name is actually Smurfette! And if I react to any of this judgment with anger or frustration then I'm validating that person's belief about Black girls named Shenequa because Shenequas are only allowed to get mad if they can contain their anger in a neat and proper fashion.

"Well, why don't you just change your name?"

The first time this suggestion was made I was living in Chicago. I was working at a small newspaper in the 'burbs and noticed the reactions of some of the locals would change after I introduced myself hoping to score an interview for a story. One Saturday at a nearby salon I let off some steam about the previous workweek. A young Black girl baring her taut stomach and pierced belly button squeezed some shampoo into her palm before rubbing it on my scalp when she made the comment.

"Do you have a middle name? Use that!" With my neck bent over a bowl forcing me to look directly into her eyes, I could tell she believed her suggestion was helpful. It wasn't.

To begin, no. Immediately, no. I won't change my name. While I've never liked the not-so-subtle changes in someone's facial expressions after introducing myself, I never felt defeated because of their reaction or so insecure about my name that I wanted to divorce myself from it. I have a deep respect for CNN journalist and author Wolf Blitzer, but his name is Wolf Blitzer. "Colorful" names are all over the place and people can and have adjusted.

A skinny kid from Chicago's South Side with big ears went on to become the forty-fourth president of the United States and his name isn't "conventional." A little Black girl from Houston, Texas, arguably became the most successful entertainer of this generation, and her name isn't traditional. (She even has an accent mark over the é.)

In 2019, a Chicago woman named Marijuana Pepsi Vandyck went viral on social media after earning her doctorate from Cardinal Stritch University in Milwaukee.[3] The topic of her dissertation? Black names in white classrooms. I was happy to see this woman proudly carry her name and not cower to society's expectations of her. She surpassed whatever limitations many may have placed on her and used what a lot of people would deem a weakness and turned it into a strength.

A year prior, I was one of several women featured in a documentary about my name. Appropriately titled *Searching for*

Shaniqua, the film highlights Black girls with "nontraditional" names like mine and how we navigate life. It was warmly received, won a few awards, and was also screened at Harvard University. During the screening I attended I realized how ironic it was that my name is what brought me to Harvard. Being named Shenequa—not Katherine, not Courtney—took me to Harvard University! About fifty people, all different gender identities, races, and backgrounds, showed up and were interested in the documentary. They shared their experiences with friends, classmates, or colleagues with different names. It was an eye-opening moment for everyone and a big "I told you so" moment for Mommy.

"See Chin, I did the right thing naming you Shenequa," Mommy said.

Mothers, mine especially, love to take credit for any of their child's accomplishments. Going to Harvard to speak on my participation in the documentary and how I choose to carry my (gorgeous) name was an achievement she would take credit for. And after penning almost five thousand words about my name, it's almost asinine that I don't give you the origin story of my nickname. When I was growing up on Oceania Street in Queens, there was a Filipino family who lived up the block from my home, and one of the sons gave me the pet name. I don't know if he couldn't pronounce Shenequa or if he was just being funny, but one day he called me Chin Chin and that name stuck to me like curry sticks to goat. Once I got older, my family started calling me Chin. I don't know how much time they're all saving by just calling me Chin instead of Chin Chin but whatevs. Chin Chin is so tattooed to my identity that when we broke the news to my then seven-year-old cousin Dallas, he didn't believe my real name is Shenequa. This family name is dear to me and if you think I hate the "Shaniqua don't live here no more" jokes, I legit turn into the Hulk when someone who doesn't know me tries to call me Chin Chin. My nickname is reserved for those who I love and love me.

As I reflected on my name, my nickname, and this chapter in general I began to wonder: What if I were *that* kind of Shenequa, the kind of Shenequa that everyone who hears my name thinks I am; would it really be that bad? On the totem pole of offenses—murder, rape, fraud, extortion, manipulation, thinking Fox is a credible news outlet, bearing false witness, actually enjoying blue cheese—if I were a Black girl who took up more room than others felt comfortable with and was a Black girl whose Black girl math always places me at a Level Eight, why would that be an issue? What's wrong with being *that* girl? What's wrong with making your presence known? Have you ever walked past a white guy talking on his cell? You can hear the conversation from down the block. He's loud as all get out, but he's not considered ghetto, but a Black girl doing the same thing is? It may not be everyone's cup of tea, I'll give you that, but that girl, that type of Shenequa, still deserves a seat at the table. It's unfair and limiting for there to be only *one* kind of Black girl, or *one* kind of Shenequa allowed in the room. I think the more Shenequas the merrier!

I'm a college graduate (with these dumbass student loans). I read lots of books and I've traveled extensively throughout Europe. I'm a little quirky (hella quirky actually) and *The Golden Girls* along with *BoJack Horseman* and *Bob's Burgers* are some of my favorite TV shows. I always cry whenever I hear Sam Cooke sing "A Change Is Gonna Come" in the fatal scene of Spike Lee's *Malcolm X.* I love jazz and I love OutKast. Like a true '90s R&B fan, I jump in the air and do the dance whenever I hear Dru Hill's "Tell Me." (I wondered if when we're jumping is that on the two and the four or the one and the three. I tweeted the question, and then Sisqó responded and said it was the one and the three . . . just an FYI.) I'll proudly knuck at the occasional buck and for, like, thirty minutes I wanted to move to Seattle because I started watching *Frasier.* If I were none of those things, and I was just Shenequa from round the way, that'd be okay too. That Black girl is just as deserving of respect. She is just as valuable.

I like my name. It's *my* name. As a woman well into her thirties, I can say Shenequa is a big name and I'm a big, bold woman. Society doesn't want me to take pride in my big girl name. Instead, I'm supposed to wilt and weaken, and it's not happening. My name fits me perfectly, and if you don't like it, that's fine, but that's your problem not mine.

So, hi! My name's Shenequa, and it's a pleasure to meet you.

2

Kimberly

As I write this chapter, Black Twitter is dissecting the idea of friendship. For the two of you alive who do not know what Black Twitter is, I'm both impressed at your ability to avoid such a large entity and a little freaked out by you as well. Black Twitter is the region of Twitter populated by Black folk in which a range of topics—Real Housewives, the healing power of ginger ale and Viola Davis, or NeNe Leakes reaction memes—are shared and discussed. Every so often, a diaspora war may break out between Black Brits, Black Africans, and Black Americans, or outrage over comments made by a guest on Power 105.1's *The Breakfast Club*, but for the most part, it's a fun place to chill and post up.

The social media examination of friendship often lacks nuance, but the arguments and opinions presented are still interesting. Black Twitter agrees friendship is vital and life-saving. Some posts have gone as far as to allege your friends can actually be your soulmate because of how rich and intimate the relationship can be. But where Black Twitter differs is what the rules of friendship are and what constitutes being a good friend, which, in a weird way, made me feel less alone. The topic of friendship has always been a touchy issue for me because, while I've had amazing friends in my life, both men and women, there's an aspect about making and maintaining friendships that I haven't mastered and feel confident about. Like most people, I picked up a lot of my social cues while in school. On the first day of kindergarten, I stole this white boy's applesauce during snack time. It was sitting there in the snack basket, so I figured yeah, why not? But he caught an attitude like a little punk and told the teacher! That's when I learned stealing snacks isn't a lucrative icebreaker. As I got older, I realized doing the little hand-dance thingy Brandy did in her "I Wanna Be Down" music video can help you catch the attention of the only other Black girl in your predominately white fourth-grade class. So, yeah, there was some trial and error and I did okay. But, as I got older, I realized a true friendship required more, and my first real life lesson in this area came by way of a girl I met in high school named Kimberly.

Okay, so let me rewind a bit. Technically, I was never a high school freshman. The awkwardness and nervousness of being a small fry in a new school with older, cooler students wasn't something I experienced, and I'll tell you why. At the time, if you went to M.S. 158 in Queens, you had the chance to either leave the middle school after completing the eighth grade and begin your freshman year at any of the neighboring high schools or finish ninth grade at 158 and start your high school career as a sophomore. I chose the latter, assuming if I bypassed the woes that come with being a freshman, I'd instantly be cool.

Yeah, no, that's not what happened at all.

I may have been able to cheat the social hierarchy by entering Benjamin N. Cardozo High School (Dozo) as a tenth grader, but I didn't know a lot of people there, and I hadn't quite shaken off my middle school vibe just yet. Camille, a childhood friend who also went to 158, opted to start her fresh-man year at Dozo. When I arrived, she welcomed me into the fold, showed me the ropes, and let me know which lunch ladies to avoid and which ones would give you extra tater tots. She was also kind enough to introduce me to the friends she made the year prior, but they still weren't *my* friends. I may have been a sophomore, but not knowing many people during those first few months in a school of almost four thousand made me feel like a freshman. That all changed one day during lunch. I walked into the cafeteria, placed my baby blue JanSport on the table, and noticed a new girl. She was short with a cinnamon complexion and apparently was also a comedienne.

"You ever be so hungry, you chew on a piece of gum and it start tasting like steak?" she quipped.

Whoever this new girl was, she quickly became a fave among everyone.

"Hi, I'm Kimberly," she said.

"Are you new here?" I asked.

"Yeah, I just transferred from Frannie Lou. You gonna give me your name or what?"

"Oh, yeah, sorry," I said with a nervous laugh. "I'm Shene-qua."

From that moment on, Kimberly and I were inseparable. Her being a new transfer and me essentially being a freshman helped make that first year bearable and sometimes fun. We leaned on one another as we navigated the emotional crazi-ness of high school and our academic workloads. Pretty soon, Camille and two other girls, Fiona and Michelle, would join us to create a proper high school clique. Kim and I spoke reg-ularly and had countless inside jokes. Every Wednesday night when *Dawson's Creek* aired, we'd dissect the show (I was team

Dawson) and then further discuss it the next day at school. We complained about our moms who "just didn't understand," shared our concerns about passing statewide exams, and, of course, talked about boys. Kimberly was the first person I told after I lost my virginity. ("When is it supposed to feel good? It is supposed to feel good, right?") And when it came time for prom, we obsessed for weeks about our dresses. ("I think I'm going to wear a gold dress, or maybe I should go for red? You think red will look nice?")

Our friendship carried us through high school and most of our twenties. We kept our bond alive during the college years despite her staying in New York and me headed to Hampton University in Virginia. Not too long after graduating, Kim received a job offer and I finished up a few credits in the summer of '07. I left Hampton and then began my journalism career as general assignment reporter for a suburban Chicago newspaper. Now, with a little more money to spend, we had more fun. We went to Puerto Rico for her twenty-fifth birthday, and the following year Kimberly and Camille came to visit me in my cramped Hyde Park studio apartment. We partied all over the city and miraculously made it home safely without me getting a DUI. (Look at God!)

I learned a lot about being a journalist, but I mostly learned I hated working inside of a newsroom. So, after three years I quit, moved back to New York, and worked at Zara during the day, and at night I applied to every editorial job I could find. On any given day before the end of my shift, Kimberly and I would make plans. We'd hit up a club or lounge on the Lower East Side, get drunk, and I'd crash at her apartment only to wake up the next morning forty-five minutes before my shift was supposed to begin. I'd rush and take the downtown 4 or 5 train, pray there wasn't a delay or some random intoxicated man trying to propose by showing me his penis, and then clock in with fifteen seconds to spare. It was a chaotic time, but it was fun. After waiting until the last minute to solidify any real New Year's Eve plans, Kim and I rang in 2011 at her place with takeout and champagne. "Happy New Year, bitches!" Kim shouted out the window. In return, she was met with a cacophony of honked horns and a few "Yerrrrrs."

Kim and I were tight, like *super tight*, yet despite the years of fun and memories we made, there was also a lot we couldn't get right and our different approach to friendship is where I, now several years removed, received my first glimpse into who I am as woman and what I can offer someone looking for friendship. A first draft of this essay was a lot of me pointing the finger at Kimberly for her "demanding" ways and my inability to speak up for myself. I was the "poor victim" and Kim, the "wicked frenemy." But after a thorough review by my editor, coupled with a gentle "Yeah, so let's rethink this," this chapter morphed into something different, more of an interrogation of friendship as a concept as opposed to an interrogation of my one-time friend.

As Kim and I got older and our respective careers started to take off, our friendship began to thin. Small fissures throughout our relationship started to crystalize. My inability to provide more emotional support after some really tough breakups stuck with her despite my apologies, and her incessant need to always communicate or make me suffer a long, cold silent treatment made my introverted self feel claustrophobic. Who we innately were as people was coming to the surface faster than she or I even knew. I didn't focus so much on our wilting relationship at the time because my career was finally taking off. I began freelancing for a media company and, all of a sudden, the world I'd been dying to get into granted me entry. One of my first opinion pieces went viral, I was interviewing celebrities left and right, and I even received an invite to the *House of Balloons* mixtape listening. I'd already heard The Weeknd's mixtape (it was kind of a big deal), but to still be invited to go for work made me feel like I'd arrived. I was also making new friends. It was easy for me to push my chilly relationship with Kimberly to the side, and, honestly, it felt like a reprieve. We'd survived our own version of cold wars before, and I had no reason to believe this would be any different. Kimberly wasn't exactly waiting by the phone for my calls either. She'd reunited with friends from college and was galivanting about town, so her social calendar was quite full.

The straw that broke our back happened a year prior to her thirtieth birthday. Kimberly began dating a guy we'll call Mitchell and like most talking stages, it went well until it didn't. She never told me what brought their situationship to an end, but Kimberly moved on and began dating someone she reconnected with from high school. During that time, Mitchell's roommate Eric and I started DMing online, flirting over the phone and seeing one another in real life. It didn't last, but Eric was cute, and I wanted to date him because I enjoy dating cute guys. (Shocker!) Kimberly, however, didn't approve, and because she didn't like or want me dating Eric, Kimberly accused me of lacking "absolute loyalty." Me, her best friend since high school and the keeper of all her secrets, had been accused of committing a friendship felony.

Kimberly was of the mindset that because things had ended badly with Mitchell, then I, as her best friend, had no business being around anyone who associated with him. How could I not know that I crossed such a blatant boundary line? And not to mention, Eric and I didn't even become a thing. So, in her mind I had risked my yearslong friendship over some dude. Joke's on me! I, however, didn't know that dating your bestie's ex-boyfriend's roommate, the man whose room was down the hall and the other signature on the lease, was such an infraction. I also didn't think I needed Kim's permission to date Eric or that Eric and I had to get married for our dating to be seen as valid. Oftentimes, if your girls don't like the guy you're seeing, and it doesn't work out, an "I told you so" or the Black woman version, "You did alladat for a man that ain't even here," is issued, and it's like, really sis? Why does every man your homegirl dates have to become her husband for the relationship to be a genuine experience and one you respect?

Kim and I had a big fight after I told her about Eric. We didn't speak for weeks and during that time I drowned in several emotions. There was guilt, because I felt like I had done something wrong; anger, because I was pissed that my loyalty and character had come into question; and confusion. Why was *this* proving to be the deciding factor in our friendship? She'd moved on from Mitchell. She'd met someone else. Why was Eric such a big deal? Yet, despite our distance, I knew her birthday was around the corner. I may have been upset about how things had left off, but I wasn't going to miss her thirtieth, so I texted her to see how she was going to spend her birthday.

Me: Hey Kim, your birthday is this Saturday. Any plans?

Kimberly: Yes. I plan to enter my thirties peaceful and burden free.[1]

Me: Sounds good, but are you going to brunch?

She never responded and it took me a minute to realize I was the "burden" that she wanted to be rid of. Days later, I saw photos of Camille and Michelle celebrating with Kimberly.

She wore a short white dress. Kimberly looked beautiful and she had celebrated a new decade with the people she wanted while everyone else was left in the past.

. . .

Friendships are important. When you're younger and your parents are getting on your nerves, you vent to your friends. When you get older and you're trying to make sense of life, it's your friends who cheer you on, help you out and catch you, God forbid, if you fall. And for Black women, our friendships are so much more; they're a sisterhood. No one protects or understands Black women like other Black women and so, for reasons bigger than us, we lean on one another and require more from each other because that support isn't something the world readily gives us. I've participated in one too many bottomless brunches with friends that bled into day parties that didn't end until midnight. I've sat in the back seat of the Uber or the Lyft, windows rolled down overlooking the New York City skyline, drunk beyond belief, laughing hysterically at God knows what with my girls. I've wiped tears from their faces, tears caused by some trash dude, and then had to bite my tongue and smile when they "worked things out." I've listened to my girls re-tell the moment they knew it was over, and then listen again when they took emotional and mental inventory of all the red flags they ignored. I've been there when new degrees were earned and when new states became home. I've held my breath, prayed, hopped on one foot, and willed into fruition the one-line/not-pregnant results after one of my friends peed on the stick. (I have peed on many a stick myself, reader.) I've willingly and lovingly extended my emotional labor to my girls because I saw them in their time of need and the same has been done for me. No one can love you like your girls.

And unfortunately, no one can hurt you deeper than your girls can.

For years, I clung to Kimberly's "absolute loyalty" comment and took her words as fact. To add insult to injury, I wondered how many other friends I had become a burden to. Was my brand of friendship too heavy to Kimberly because she felt she wasn't getting what she was giving? Was I not meeting her halfway? But then I had to question was I "easier to carry" all the times I obliged *her* requests? Was I loyal whenever I did things *her* way? I told my mom about Kim and her comment, and she wondered if Kimberly was secretly in witness protection and if her last name was actually Capone.

"What is she, a mob boss? Who is she to demand absolute loyalty from anyone?"

Point taken, Mommy.

Losing a friend is a different kind of grief and mourning. Even if you know deep in the marrow of your bones the loss is for the best, it still hurts. At some point, as a young (hetero-sexual) woman, you learn that boys come and go for myriad reasons, but your girls are supposed to be forever. Over time, your girlfriends become a safety net of sorts. Have a bad day at work? Call your girls. Your toxic family getting on your nerves? Call your girls. That one boy you like starts acting funny by not returning text messages so now you *have* to become Redd Foxx, call your girls. When that safety is removed for whatever reason, the emotional free fall is breathtaking. My breakup with Kim happened shortly before I turned thirty and since then I've made a slew of friends and lost some as well. Each case was different but none as deep as the "divorce" from Kim. When we parted ways, I cried hard and I cried a lot, but I also felt like I finally took my bra off after more than a decade. It was a mix-ture of "I love you, but girl, kick rocks!" A physical relief came over me. The tension, the discomfort, and the responsibility of always having to fulfill what felt like her never-ending needs was no longer a requirement of mine. I didn't have to always be at attention anymore and I loved it. But then it dawned on me: If I felt relief after saying goodbye to her, did she feel the same way about me? Was our time as friends only supposed to carry us into our third decade of life or did we both lack the proper skills to make our love story last longer?

I've been fortunate enough to not have experienced much death in my life. Over the course of a decade or so, I lost three uncles all for different reasons. Their passings were shocking and tragic, but I wasn't close with them, so I logically understood what was happening, but I emotionally wasn't as affected as I could've been. When Kimberly and I parted ways, that was my first real encounter with a kind of death and the emotional toll it can take. That grief lingered for years, but what I didn't know was happening was that Kimberly's exit from my life had watered my loner seed. I've always been okay with being alone (more on this in subsequent chapters), but after Kim, that distant feeling of being "by myself" was pushed to the fore. Kimberly taught me that relationships can come to an end and in the end all I have is me. You couldn't tell twenty-something Shenequa that Kimberly wasn't always going to be in her life. That wasn't even a thought. Now I know otherwise, and this knowledge has clogged how much love and water I can give to relationships. In the back of my mind, I know there is no future in forever, so I will cherish you now but I'm withholding parts of me because when you leave, you won't take all of me with you.

The trauma responses that blossom from friendships deferred are just as deep as the ones brought on from family drama and abusive romantic relationships, but for whatever reason, they're not given their proper bouquet of flowers. Why do we discredit the hurt that comes from losing a friend or a friendship taking on a new looser shape, devoid of the closeness it once had? Are we so limited as a society that we believe that lasting intimacy can only be shared with sexual partners? Carrie Bradshaw once questioned after a breakup, where does the love go? In regard to dead friendships, I wonder the same and would add, where does the grief go? The laughs? The joy? The "Girl, 'memba that one time at Harlem Tavern with the waiter who had the crazy hairline and he kept winking at you and refilling your water?" I can go visit my uncles' tombstones if I want. I can place fresh flowers and weep and wonder how old they would've been had they lived. What jokes would they tell? Would they be team iPhone or Android? There is no emotional cemetery for dead friendships. There's no place where I can review the length of our time together, honor what was had, return to it during the spring when flowers bloom or in the autumn to wipe away the leaves that have fallen. There's just silence, our hurt, pride, and the blocked button on social media.

There also isn't enough conversation about how friendships change with age and how that change can also feel like a death. We're not in high school anymore. We can't gossip or catch up in the hallways while you're headed to calculus and I'm on my way to the locker room for gym. We have more physical responsibilities that must be tended to. We literally don't have the *time* to be the kind of friend we wish we could or once were. The obvious counter is "You make time for the things you value, right?" Sure, but haven't you always wanted to learn a new language or travel to Hawaii or clean out your closet? The physical wear and tear from working coupled with the emotional one-two punch of life makes watering anything other than a houseplant feel like another chore or responsibility. The idea of chillin' with your girls, going to brunch, or seeing a movie should feel invigorating, but for a lot of people already having to give so much everywhere else, friendships, the one lifeline that shouldn't get cut, is often cut first. It's not fair. It's not right, but it happens.

. . .

I'm well into my thirties now, equipped with lower back pains and health insurance I don't use nearly as much as I should. I now have a better understanding of who I am and what I can offer as a friend. And a lot of these lessons were learned after meeting and having better friends than Kimberly. I can and will be there for you. I can listen to you. I can hug you when you cry, grab the tissues to wipe your tears, and then reapply and properly blend out the concealer that was messed up in the process. (If you're lucky, I may even have my travel-size Huda Beauty Easy Bake loose setting powder in my purse.) I'll cuss out ol' dude for you and then help dismember the body, freeze it, and then dispose of it in a wooded area a year later so investigators can't really narrow down a time of death. We can go to brunch; we can make a Target run. We can have emotional and mental realizations about life and our childhood and how we were raised. I've got jokes all day, sis! We can spend the time. We can get cupcakes. I can help you with your issues. We can discuss it once, twice, three times if necessary.

But come the fourth time, I need you to help yourself.

I do not have the emotional bandwidth or desire to continue to hear the same story fifty million times, because my brand of friendship requires a level of self-sufficiency on your part. I am not a couch for my friends to throw their woes on, deposit their "emotional crumbs" within the cushions, and, when they're feeling better, get up and leave. I'm the friend who will support you and homeboy the first go-round. I'll even give a half-hearted smile during the Ryan Coogler–directed sequel, but if you want to continue to give homeboy a chance despite him proving he's traumatizing to your well-being, then best of luck to you, baby girl, but you're on your own.

Like most people, I need a listening ear and a truthful tongue. I need you to understand that I'm down for a lunch date, but I'll also need to be home at a decent enough hour to recharge by myself. My alone time doesn't mean I don't love you. It's how I say "I love you" to myself. I can't be the only one to share funny gifs, memes, and TikToks. Laughter is a love language, and I am proficient, and I need you to be fluent as well. I'll have a drink with you, but don't force me to have more than one if I don't want to. Peer pressure doesn't just happen in high school. It also happens with adults, and I'm done hearing how lame I am simply because I won't join you in your fifth old-fashioned or your third shot.

As an adult, I understand better than ever that life is fragile and can be lonely. Between the ages of thirty-three and, say, forty-seven, the world stops paying attention to you by means of music, entertainment, and advertisements and you're kind of left to your own devices. But it's during this time the most life happens. You can legit meet your spouse, get pregnant, have a baby, lose some of your hair during postpartum (it happens), buy a house, have a cancer scare, lose a parent, get divorced, fight like hell for full custody of the kids and the Peloton in the divorce proceedings, and be expected to handle it all on your own because you're "grown." But if you don't have a solid network of friends, you'll drown. That's not hyperbole. That's fact. If you want a fighting chance at a happy life, you need friends; the trick is balancing friendships with life's constant demands.

One of the biggest lies *Sex and the City* ever told wasn't Carrie Bradshaw's lavish lifestyle despite being a freelance writer or negotiating four dollars a word while writing a piece for *Vogue* (which is indeed a flex); it was the fact that these four very different and dynamic women had time every week to go to brunch. I have a friend who's a general manager and another who's a director and one who's starting their own consulting business. It took three tries to finally meet up for dinner at a Creole restaurant downtown. Seeing your friends every week does not happen in real life, and it should, maybe not weekly, but it should happen regularly, because you need that sense of community. You must till the soil of your friendships both in the good and bad times because there will be moments in life when there is no place you can walk, cry, and feel safe except for the garden you and your girlfriends created. When I was going through the thick of it with Redacted, it was my close friend Grace who wiped my tears and fed me stale tater tots at some nearby dive bar.

Wait. Who's Redacted?

Next chapter, boo. Next chapter.

I haven't seen or spoken to Kimberly in some time. I don't know what she's up to, whether she's married, a mom, or taken up pottery. And as I type this, I also realize I have no desire to check in and find out. There was a time I wanted Kimberly to trip into oncoming traffic while holding a partially opened jar of red tomato sauce. I didn't have gentle feelings toward her. But I've gotten to a better space. The word "boundary" has become a thing in the last five or seven years. The idea that this line, whatever and wherever that line is, should not be crossed is easy to put in practice with colleagues and strangers on the street but feels idiotic and almost rude when it comes to family and friends. Love has always been positioned as something you give consistently and with unfiltered access. To prohibit those you care for from being fully in your space, occupying all of your time, and using all of your resources, has previously been viewed as showing a lack of love. Now, more evolved, some of us know better and understand. Kimberly helped me define my boundaries within a friendship. She helped me figure out who I am, what I can give, and where I have to draw the line. Most importantly, my fallout with "Kimberly Capone" helped me define me. I didn't like *how* she did it, but she did assist.

3

Redacted

"So, that's why I couldn't get in contact with you?" my friend Harry said. "I was textin' you and I thought you ghosted ya boy, on some 'new year new me' type energy."

Harry played it off like he didn't feel a way, but I could tell he was hurt. It had been a few weeks, maybe even a month, since we last spoke and after several attempts at trying to contact me, I understood why he assumed my silence was avoidance. Harry and I are close friends with a pretty consistent flow of communication, so for me to fall off the face of the earth was peculiar. We met about seven years ago at La Liñea to celebrate a friend's birthday. The Lower East Side lounge is a staple in the city and boasted strong cheap drinks, clean-ish couches back when standing on couches in the club was a thing, and a DJ who played the music we grew up listening to on *106 & Park*. (More so when A.J. and Free were hosts, not the Julissa and Big Tigger years.) Harry walked in wearing a bucket hat and made a beeline to the back where he sat on the arm of a loveseat. Before a man's beard became a sign of luxury and faux emotional development, Harry's facial hair was full, shiny, and impressive, an apparent byproduct of his Philadelphia upbringing. Before the night's end, we were the best of friends.

"I had to change my number," I said sheepishly over the phone. "Redacted refused to stop calling and texting, and if I'm being honest, I didn't want him to have access to me."

"Did you try blocking him first?" Harry questioned.

"Of course I tried, but he would just call from another number and the harassment would begin all over again," I said.

"I'm sorry. I know men have a hard time letting go sometimes, but I didn't know ol' boy caused you to change your number because of it."

In April 2020, after repeatedly telling Redacted to stop calling, I bit the bullet, contacted my cell phone provider, and explained why I was making the change. As a result, the compassionate representative didn't charge me the supposed fee that comes with getting a new number and the new life that comes with it.

"Neek, let me hit you back. I have to take this call," Harry said.

"Okay, don't forget to save my new number," I said hastily before he hung up.

"I got you," Harry promised.

For about ten years, friends, family, colleagues, doctors and dentist's offices, hell, even Sallie Mae reps could reach me at my old 9-1-7 number. I liked my phone number because it had a certain bounce to it, and it was easy to remember, plus, the last four digits allowed your thumb to do a little fun hopscotch thingy when dialing it into the keypad. I didn't realize how attached I was to my phone number until I had to give it up. I also didn't factor in how drastic a change it would be once I did. Getting a new number is the digital equivalent to moving. It's more than just a different sequence of digits for people to use to get in contact with you. It's a lifestyle change. Your phone number, in a lot of ways, also adds to your identity. For older millennials like myself, we grew up sharing a telephone with everyone who lived in our house. If a friend or, God forbid, a boy called, you and the person had to time the call perfectly so you'd pick up the phone and not someone else. Shouting, "I got it!" or "It's for me" was a common way to carve out even the slightest bit of independence. But in the event an adult answered when the phone rang, your friend would have to *speak* to the elder in the house. I want to take a moment to acknowledge how important this is in hindsight. A brief conversation would ensue in which the guardian or parent would use that small encounter to sniff out any potential foolery over the phone. So manners, respect, and a soft voice were imperative. We didn't know it then, but a lot of the phone etiquette older millennials still have today and the breathtaking ability to deal with airline customer service representatives, comes from having to speak to somebody's no-nonsense mama or grandmama when we were kids.

Before cell phones, memorizing your home phone number or your parent's office number was an active safety measure school officials stressed to children. My old house number rolls off my tongue because it's still nestled in my heart, despite not having lived on Oceania Street in more than twenty years. Phone numbers, as commonplace as they are, also hold a significant emotional space for each of us. My cousin Tisha (pronounced tee-SHA) has had the same 9-1-7 number for at least twenty-five years, and she would die before ever changing it. Tisha's attachment to her number isn't an anomaly. There are many people whose livelihoods are fastened to others getting in contact with them, and after years of building a robust Rolodex, the admin work to convert all those names over to a new number is too much. Conversely, whenever tensions arise within relationships, individuals attempting to showcase how

unafraid or willing they are to settle the matter will say something to the effect of: "You coulda hit my line. My number ain't
change." The permanence of one's phone number is intended
to crush the flimsiness of the argument, and to highlight the
supposed cowardice of the offender.

Growing up, *Moesha* was one of the flyest Black girls on
television. Her clothes were always on point, her braids were
fresh, and Q's fine ass was feeling her, but Moesha also had
a phone in her room, which allowed for her personal life to
be more real. That's what my cell phone gave me. When I got
my first phone, an ice-blue brick Nokia, a whole new world of
autonomy became available to me. There was no such thing as
self-governance growing up in a multigenerational West Indian household, and privacy was too ripe a space for something
inappropriate to occur, or so I was led to believe. With my own
cell phone, suddenly, I was *grown*. I could give my number
to boys and not create a reasonable enough excuse when they
called the house or worry about a suspicious auntie noticing my
giggles. Initially, I tried to play it off. I'd be all *It's just a phone.
No big deal*, trying to hide my excitement behind faux measured
coolness, and then the moment I received a call I would run,
jump, cartwheel, backflip, and somersault just to answer it. It
was an all-out Dominique Dawes floor routine. I was so hyped
somebody was calling *my* phone. I now had a life outside of the
one constantly monitored by the adults in my life. It was new,
exciting, and it was freeing.

I've had several phone numbers over the course of my adult
life, but I changed those numbers because I wanted to, not
because someone was harassing me. At the tail end of 2019,
Redacted and I started dating. Hour-long phone conversations quickly turned into lunch dates in Dumbo or walking
hand in hand in Harlem. We'd known one another for about

five years before anything romantic happened, and I foolishly assumed our time as friends meant I'd be treated with
a higher regard. (Let's all hold hands and laugh together,
shall we?) Redacted is thin and brown-skinned with a smile
made perfect from years of braces. His accent tickled, like
when a man's mustache dances across a woman's upper lip
during a kiss. He could quote Ghostface in one breath and
Professor Eddie Glaude in the next. He belonged to and felt
comfortable in both worlds. Once we went to The Strand, a
landmark bookstore for readers, writers, introverts, extroverts, and anyone who knows that books are the best thing
ever in life. There he introduced me to the "Michael Jordan
of Civil War books," Shelby Foote. Whenever he leaned into
his academic side, I was at a loss. I tried my best to offer up
a sincere smile that I hoped my furrowed eyebrows didn't
give away. He'd go on and on about why certain academics
were great while others were simply trying to impress other
academic colleagues. Again, I'd just nod and smile, and said,
"Okay, babe!"

For a brief moment, there was possibility and maybe even
hope. Hope that the one I'd been wishing for was right under my nose, but as fast as our relationship started is as fast
as it ended. The goodness between us was short-lived, about
the length of movie previews, but the fallout commenced for
what felt like the duration of a standard film. In "normal"
relationships, you deal with sucky breakups in your individual corners of the earth. Maybe you reread the text messages
sent during better times and wonder if there's a chance for
a part two. Or maybe you let off a few shady subtweets, but
that should be the extent of it. You cry. You mope around
the house, but eventually you get over things, slowly at first,
maybe really slowly, depending on how the breakup was

carried out (or if you're a Cancer), but you do get on with your life. This wasn't the case. Instead, an inflated ego watered by a decade-long drug addiction implored Redacted to harass me relentlessly.

Many people mentioned within these pages are given fake names. For legal purposes, yes, but also to protect their privacy. A lot of this book is a look back at my life, my choices, and the people in it at various times, and despite how evolved and mature I thought I was, or we'd like to think we are, there are many moments that prove otherwise. Some people who I no longer speak to are still deserving of that grace by way of anonymity. That isn't the case here. The reason why this person is referred to as Redacted isn't to protect his identity. It's to fully hold him accountable for his multiple emotional felonies, while stripping him of the dignity and power that come with saying his name. His name is stricken from the record, yes, but the record, along with the hurt and fear he caused, still remains. He was a part of my life, and as embarrassing as it is to admit it, I invited him into my orbit. Starved for love, affection, and tenderness, I brought him in. The ripple effect from that decision is most prominently felt in the fact that I changed my phone number and the emotional price I had to pay afterward. I couldn't predict the blowback that I would experience after getting a new number. I assumed it would be an easy relationship to sever, but it was so much more than that. I can't take back the choice I made; all I can do is pull from it to write this chapter. So, here goes.

The first text message after our breakup came by way of our mutual friend Brittany in March 2020. She reached out to tell me he wanted to talk. I wanted nothing to do with him and informed her to deliver that message. Advocating for Redacted or simply not wanting to be in the middle of our mess, Brittany advised the best way to handle this was to be stern while expressing my wishes and need for distance. On the surface, this mini–pep talk seemed sincere, like she understood where I was coming from or had been through it herself. But after a beat, I became annoyed. Redacted sent his friend to do a temperature check, and the thermometer reading proved there was no heat left in our affair. This brief touch-base, if you will, felt like a shallow attempt at empathizing with me. It was insulting and minimized *why* we came to an end.

Redacted's constant legal woes and the mounting stress they placed on our relationship sucked all the kisses, cuddles, and happiness out of us and thus led to our demise. Brittany knew this, which made this check-in feel like the emotional equivalent to "just following up on the below email" after the three-day Memorial Day weekend. Being a "ride or die" girlfriend never sounded appealing or romantic, and I've never had to ride or die in any other relationship, so why would I start now? To send a friend to do his bidding was too trivial a play for how and why our relationship ended. Redacted and I didn't collapse because of miscommunication or cheating, which could arguably merit this kind of olive branch.

Despite expressing my demands to Brittany, he still called. I silenced my phone and watched the number scroll across the screen. The beauty of cell phones is that they allow your passive-aggressive Patty (or Patrick) to thrive. I wondered if my own inner Patty had taken the reins. Was I passing off my responsibility onto Brittany to communicate something I was too afraid to say myself? Fun fact: I'm not the best at confrontation. Rarely, if ever, have I seen two people effectively communicate how they strongly feel without voices being raised and things being said that can't be taken back. Restraint, if exercised, is usually considered a weakness during discord. Being the bigger person sounds great in theory, but in practice it requires twice as much strength. One gallon of energy to withstand the person's attacks and then another to let the assault go. Most people don't have conflict resolution skills; they just resolve to win the conflict, your feelings be damned, which is why aggression and disrespect during confrontation is often believed to be the best weapon of defense.

As Redacted's number scrolled across my screen, I froze until it stopped and then let out a sigh of relief when I received the missed call notification. I felt safer knowing he tried but couldn't reach me, like I protected myself with silence. After the call ended, I put my phone on Do Not Disturb, placed my locs within my silk bonnet, fluffed my pillow, and waited for sleep.

A month later he contacted me again.[1]

REDACTED: Hey Shenequa, this is Redacted.
Do you have a minute to talk please?

And please don't call my friends
and tell them I texted you.

Just say no or ignore the text.

It was April 2020 and New York City was the epicenter for the COVID-19 pandemic. Governor Andrew Cuomo gave briefings on new cases and the daily death toll, which were often as high as six or seven hundred. Dr. Anthony Fauci was as big of a celebrity as Beyoncé, and sirens from ambulances shuttling people to emergency rooms could be heard in every neighborhood across the country. Nurses and doctors were either considered heroes or villains depending on who you spoke to, and living suddenly became confined. There was little concrete information about the virus, but its effects were immediate. I was in my room in the middle of a Zoom meeting when I received the text. Redacted had a new number, this time with a 6-4-6 area code, and it took my brain half a second to process who it was from, and the request being made. At first, anxiety washed over me and then soon after rage. He wanted my time and attention but was bold enough to instruct me on what *not* to do.

> REDACTED: Please don't call my friends and tell them I texted you. Just say no or ignore the text.

I try to remind myself there's a difference between men and toxic men. Lumping them in a pile together isn't fair or accurate. Decent men hear a woman's no and about-face. While their ego and feelings may be bruised, their pride won't allow them to show it, and the idea of not being wanted or being perceived as a creep is enough motivation to send them on their way. Toxic men, however, don't care about how women feel or what they say. Women are to be owned, and anything outside of full submission to whatever the request, even a phone call, results in imaginative displays of audacity.

I sat in my room contemplating how many more text messages or phone calls I would have to receive before Redacted respected my request. Would it be one, ten, or one hundred? Would they come weekly, pop up like an unexpected pimple, or be more regimented like a monthly menstrual? My phone, which doubled as a tool for communication and a source of distraction whenever I was bored, quickly became the portal that Redacted used to remain connected to me. The one saving grace was he never came to my house. While I would spend that night at his Harlem apartment, he never stayed at mine as I lived with Mommy at the time, and my Jamaican mother could care less how grown I was or the fact that I paid half the rent; she was not interested in any sort of sleepovers in her home. But as long as I had that phone number, Redacted had access to me and could infringe on my peace whenever he chose. Whether I was out to dinner, at the movies, cleaning my bathroom, or watching a YouTube makeup tutorial, if Redacted wanted to, he could disturb me.

"Do you think I should change my number?" I asked my friend Ashleigh. "One month went by and I thought I was in the clear only for Redacted to reach out again."

"Hmm." Ashleigh said. "Changing your number is your choice, but that's a big change, mama. Your job and ability to get freelancing opportunities are attached to that number. New editors send an email, which is fine, but the ones who really rock with you usually drop a text, no?"

"I didn't even think about that, Ash," I said, defeated. "Good God! Why won't he just leave me alone? It's really not that hard."

I was annoyed about potentially slowing my freelance work down, but deeper than that I was beginning to understand the severity of it all. It suddenly hit me that I was the one who had to change and sacrifice a part of me just to merit some peace from him. Redacted was unwilling to give me the space I deserved or asked for simply because he didn't want to. He hadn't bought my phone and didn't pay my bill, yet here I was contemplating changing my number because he refused to give me the distance I needed. He inflicted the wound and now wanted me, by way of access and communication, to allow him to infect it. Yes, people change their numbers and addresses all the time for all sorts of reasons. A simple mass text or email can be sent out informing family, friends, colleagues and that's that, but I was being forced to do this because a man refused to acquiesce to a request. Do you know how easy it is to *not* call someone?

"Do you really want to give that up?" Ashleigh questioned.

I knew Ashleigh meant no harm by her question. No one was more acutely aware of Redacted and all of his shenanigans than she and our other close friend Grace. In the beginning of our relationship, Ash and Grace cheered us on during the romantic times, and like good girlfriends, they willingly contributed to the "You know, I never really liked fam, not even gon' hold you. I 'memba that one time . . . " hymnal that's often sung when true colors are shown. Yet during our call when Ashleigh said "give it up," it felt like she was blaming me, like I wasn't putting up a hard-enough fight for my phone number and the life I'd built using it. Yet despite my bruised feelings, her words still echoed. Did getting a new number mean Redacted won? This boxing ring we'd entered into, with him in one corner bloated with entitlement and me in the other corner having to fight for my peace and privacy, filled my already cluttered brain.

And then, out of nowhere, stubbornness joined me for a drink as I strategized solutions. I'd had my number for ten years. I wasn't changing it because of *him*! I could potentially tire him out and block every text or call I received, disengaging whenever he made contact, but that still put me on the defense with my own phone. I didn't want to be scared whenever I received a notification or missed call, but that's exactly where I was and how I felt. My phone suddenly had become a tool that Redacted could use to revictimize me whenever he felt like it and I wanted my power and privacy back. When you give someone your phone number you're giving them more immediate and intimate access to you. It's the equivalent of meeting someone for dinner versus inviting them over. I had let

Redacted into my space, and trying to get him out was proving way more challenging than I could've imagined.

But in retrospect, it was foolish of me to assume I could go back to the life I had before I "invited him over." When new people enter your world, whether friends or lovers, you change. Maybe not drastically, but you shed a little skin, because you're participating in something different, and whatever lesson or experience that person teaches can stick to you or change you. I couldn't verbalize it then, but there was no way I could return to the Shenequa of old. That girl with the old 9-1-7 number no longer existed, and in deciding to change my number, I was not only giving up a digital piece of my identity, but just below the surface I knew I was formally saying goodbye to a girl who didn't deserve to be let go. She was a friend and now had become a casualty, and I was burying her before her time.

It took twenty minutes to get rid of my old number and reprogram my phone with a new one. The agent gave me a menu of available options. There was a 7-1-8 number, but I haven't been a 7-1-8 girl since my mid-twenties and everything about my twenties was tears, impressively low credit scores, and skinny jeans. There was a 6-4-6 option that looked cute, but Redacted texted me from a 6-4-6 number so there's that. There was a 5-1-6 number, and no, just no. My mom has a 3-4-7 number, but every other area code felt like tried-and-true New York, and the 3-4-7s of the world always seemed like the little cousin you're forced to play with. I settled on a 9-1-7 number that stuck out to me. The number flows, it's easy to remember, and, oddly enough, I felt like it could grow on me.

About an hour into my relationship with my new phone number, the clerical work of informing folks began. After telling my family, I texted Ashleigh and Grace and asked to be added back to the WhatsApp group chat. I hit up my former roommate Chris and then a few old colleagues I had developed a good rapport with. I then informed everyone at my job and updated my online banking information, contacted a few editors who often reached out about freelancing opportunities, and made sure my doctors and dentist had my most updated information. I texted my therapist my new number and knew before our next session was fully booked what the topic of discussion would be. (*So, Shenequa, new boundaries, yeah?*) I knew I was forgetting a few people, but the most important had my number and that was good enough. Everyone who needed to know now knew. All of this took about an hour or so, and thankfully I didn't have to out myself or my reasons in the process. No one asked why the switcheroo took place and I was thankful. My network's nonchalance in regard to the matter acted as a weird confirmation that I had done the right thing. People change their numbers all the time. It's not like there's a sign on your forehead that reads "Entitled Ex-Boyfriend Harassing You. Change Number Now."

Jumping into the group chat and getting into the day's social media gossip with Ashleigh and Grace made me feel normal. That first night I went to bed with my new number, I was overcome with a sense of security. I had permanently removed someone from my life, and while the sacrifice was big, the peace of mind that soon followed was worth it. Sure, I'd have to reach out to a few more people and bear the "who's this?" response, but things could be worse. I could have anxiety over every voicemail left on my phone or every unsaved number texting me, but that wasn't the case anymore. I had freed myself from Redacted and prohibited him from having any control over my life. I took my power back and that night slept soundly.

Two months later I received an email.

Subject Line: YO, I HOPE YOU GET THIS![2]

"I deadass hate you. I really do hate
you. I literally hate you."

The body of the message was a manic display of a man coming undone and blaming me for his unraveling. Whatever woes he had worked toward now came knocking on his door, but somehow, I was the one responsible. And after reading the email I quickly ballooned with defeat. I had changed my number because I didn't want Redacted to have any access to me only for him to email me everything he couldn't say via a text message or a call. I'd had my personal email address for twice as long as I'd had my old 9-1-7 number, and I couldn't change it. I wouldn't! It held way too much important information. It was my digital mailbox. Once again, I was up against the ropes because seemingly after Redacted tried to text again, he realized he couldn't and then he used the next best form of communication he had. My sense of safety and privacy was shattered again! This wasn't just a hurt man. This was someone furious about being emotionally demoted. I blocked the email address just like I had blocked his phone number, and then a month later, he emailed me again from a new address. And so, it went for about a year. Every month or two Redacted would create a new email address and email me some accusation about why I was the reason his life was in peril. One muggy August night, I received about ten to twelve angry and chaotic emails ranging from "help me" to "how could you?" He wanted me to save him, while I was trying to save myself *from* him.

Redacted was my first introduction to addiction. I'd heard stories and watched enough documentaries to know how damaging any addiction could be to the person and their loved ones. I knew it was a disease and should be handled with care, but how that disease manifested—by way of harassment, flashes of anger and blame—made my empathy for him run cold. It's fascinating actually. In his mind, I was supposed to tolerate everything and love him as if none of what happened had occurred. Yet, even in his anger, Redacted couldn't see his privilege. While he threw his tantrums and behaved badly, I remained calm. His conduct proved there was no boundary he wouldn't cross, and no consequence too great. Redacted didn't have anything to lose, which meant there wasn't anything I'd win by engaging with him. Did he have a problem? Yes. Was he deserving of treatment and care? Of course. But was his problem supposed to free him from his wrongdoing? No. You have an addiction so now I have to put up with your inability to not contact me? Again, I say: Do you know how easy it is to *not* call someone?

Over the last few years, conversations about mental health have bubbled. Many are beginning to see and value the importance of speaking with a trained counselor to make sense of their emotions, trace their origins, and find practical solutions for their life. What I've noticed is a subset of the mental health conversations has been the weaponization of emotional qualities. About five years ago, it felt like forgiveness, what it means and why it's important, was thrust into the public eye. Forgiveness became the emotional safety net we were told we needed to be mature individuals and live in a more harmonious society. You have hurt people, people have hurt you, forgive and be forgiven. But how is one to forgive the actions of an offender who has not shown even a dollop of remorse or is still actively offending?

Forgiveness finished its Coachella set and then sympathy and empathy, the Tia and Tamera of the wellness community, took center stage. Putting yourself in the other person's shoes and suspending your judgment to see their point of view and understand what they're feeling is a phenomenal quality, but how far should my empathy extend? How am I supposed to forgive a man who's more concerned with his ego than my request for distance? How much more emotional labor must I carry just to be made whole again? By extending forgiveness, sympathy, and empathy, it felt like more work on top of the hurt I already had to work through and the wounds he kept infecting with his constant communication. If I were a gambling gal, I'd put my money on grace becoming the new hot emotional quality that will be weaponized. Everybody's going through fifty-leven things all at once, so yes, grace *must* be given. We have to let people be human and be imperfect and give them the room to make mistakes without bringing down the hammer on folks every single time, but how much grace should be given before accountability is served? Will we be giving folks grace or are we giving people more space for their mistreatment of us to frolic? After about a year and some change, all communication stopped. I don't know what did it, but I'd like to believe he finally got sober, which means my life became easier.

According to the National Intimate Partner and Sexual Violence Survey, one in three women have been stalked at some point in their lives, and in 2011, the National Center on Violence Against Women in the Black Community reported that nearly 20 percent of Black women have experienced stalking in their lifetime.[3] Some may assume a few unwanted emails and text messages don't constitute anything other than a nuisance. And I say to you, why did I receive unwanted emails and calls after making my stance clear at all? My desire to be left alone wasn't outside of his skill set. What's even more fascinating is that so many people are unaware that the distance between ignoring a woman's "no" and stalking or killing her isn't a giant leap.

I've experienced breakups in which you see the person in a year, maybe two, and you're able to have a civil conversation. It's brief, full of the tact and politeness used by former lovers who've gotten over the hurt and don't want to return to it, because sometimes seeing your ex reminds you of how far you've come. One spring day while driving with my mom, I glanced in the rearview mirror and saw a man who resembled Redacted. Fear washed over me. Another glance and I realized it wasn't him and my racing heart began to settle. Which begs the question: What would I do if I ran into him? Would I freeze? Cry? Scream? What would you do if someone proved to you that consequence is of no consequence to them?

I went back and forth about whether I should write this chapter. He hasn't contacted me in some time and I'm thankful every day for that silence and peace. Out of fear of poking the bear, I wondered if remaining silent was best. I also didn't want to give his ashy ass any kind of validation. This is *my* book; why should he take up any space? Well, it's because he's shaped me. Two years after Redacted, I began seriously dating this Gemini from East New York. (I know, I know, Gemini men are ridiculous, but he was chill.) He's a sneakerhead and tried to slowly welcome me into the fold. One day, I asked him to buy me a pair of Air Max 97s (I'd never had a pair) and he obliged. Naturally, he needed my address to send them to me, and when he asked for it, I freaked.

Wait, then he'll know where I lay my head.

What if things go sideways?

Will he harass me like Redacted?

Will he show up at my house?

Things are good now, but who knows how he'll act if we break up?

Before Redacted, I knew in theory that some guys can be dangerous. Now, I know in practice just how dangerous they can be, and more so than changing my number, I was left with a hypervigilance that's heavy to bear but necessary to carry. It's become my own personal firearm if you will. I've turned a large part of myself into stone as a means of protection. I cannot easily smile, chat, or even flirt with a man I think is cute out of fear that potentially liking or loving him will result in me losing something else. It's more than just my phone number, y'all. It's about having my peace, privacy, and, as a byproduct, my safety not respected. You operate differently when you know someone can become unhinged simply because you told them no.

. . .

Fast-forward to April 2022. It was a gorgeous spring day. I found a dress in my closet I bought maybe five years before and never wore and I was even more thrilled when I tried it on and it still fit. The elation quickly dissipated once I realized I was about to miss my train because I hadn't finished my makeup. After furiously blowing on the lash glue and popping on the falsies, I threw my lipstick and liner in my purse, grabbed my coat, and made it to the station in just enough time to see my train headed to Brooklyn ride off into the distance. "Damn the man!" I said to myself. I raced up the concrete stairs (in thigh-high boots, might I add) only to miss my train and work up a sweat. I texted my friends to let them know I'd be late and as I placed my iPhone back into my jacket pocket, I felt something. Retrieving it, I realized it was a card from Redacted from when he bought me flowers. It read:

Cookie Monster,
Here's a small gift to hopefully help you feel good. That's it.[4]

Cookie Monster was his nickname for me. I looked at this card, reread his chicken scratch handwriting, and felt . . . nothing. Not anger, sadness, disgust, rage for all the disruption he had caused. Nothing.

I questioned if that was the truest sign of growth or healing after a deep wound had been inflicted? If so, I'll take it.

4

A September Kiss

We were in Dumbo when Stephen called an Uber. He had to get back to his hotel, which meant our date would end soon. We ate some bad boneless wings at a nearby Mexican restaurant, and the waitress seemed more shocked Stephen asked for two ginger ales and not two margaritas. After dinner, we walked to a park and sat on a bench overlooking the Manhattan Bridge. A man with a canvas and easel was painting the picturesque cityscape while onlookers admired the beauty in both his artwork and the actual bridge. The sun, just beginning to set, illuminated everything. It was early September and while summer wasn't quite letting go of its grasp, autumn was making its presence known with a faint breeze.

It made more sense for me to walk back to the train and head home. I was about thirty minutes away from my then Crown Heights apartment, but I hadn't worked up the courage to kiss him yet, so into the Uber I went. I couldn't tell you the last time a man stopped me in my tracks the way Stephen did. Don't get me wrong; I know men exist, but Stephen did something to me. He had a sex appeal that was hidden just below his quiet confidence. Standing well above six feet tall, his full lips and almond-shaped eyes made it difficult for me not to stare. His broad shoulders gave him presence and while he had what some may consider a scowl, his toothy boyish smile and chubby cheeks were enough to calm any nerves, including mine.

Stephen appeared unshakeable, like he never doubted himself. (He's a Leo, so there's that.) He was kind and a great conversationalist, which made him even sexier. I can't tell you how many times I've met men who don't know how to form complete sentences, much less hold up their end of a conversation. Stephen, on the other hand, could go on for days about politics, anime, or whatever topic was on the table. We'd met a month prior, exchanged numbers, and because I'm timid when it comes to dating, instead of simply telling him I thought he was gorgeous and I wanted to get to know him more, I reverted to asking fifty-leven questions. Everything from "How do you feel about runny eggs?" to "Aside from Wolverine (because everyone loves Wolverine) who's your favorite X-Man?"—mentally adding extra points if he liked Nightcrawler or Cyclops from the comics. My curiosity has always been the strongest indicator of my attraction.

I didn't know if Stephen was sincerely interested in me or if he was just bored, but I wanted and needed proof that I could be lusted after by a man I lusted for. As a woman walking from point A to point B in New York City, you'd be hard-pressed to not receive any number of catcalls from dudes shooting their shot for sport, which made me feel like genuine reciprocity was a luxury, not a guarantee or a right. And for me, it was such a rarity that I started viewing it as a fairytale. I wanted to know *that* part of me still "worked," that my feminine side, if activated by the type of guy I was into, could merit the attention I wanted. I was tired of having to pick from the leftover litter of dudes. I wanted first dibs.

We were in the Uber when, in the middle of his sentence, I finally "womaned" up.

"May I kiss you?" I asked.

"Yes," he replied.

Stephen cupped my face with his hands and used his lips to massage mine. I may have been the one who initiated the ask, but he quickly took the lead in the rhythm of it all. (Remember, he's a Leo.) He wasn't slow nor did he rush. Some guys think sticking their tongue down your throat will make their album go platinum. I've never enjoyed that and Stephen, thankfully, didn't do that. Our mouths were in a delicate dance and just as I assumed we perfected our two-step, his left hand made its way to my neck and while still kissing me, he tightened his grip just so. The mix of pleasure and pain was unexpected and titillating.

Kisses have always been important to me. Before I began having sex, kisses were the only physical connection I had with a guy. Hugs were whatever, and holding hands was okay, but kisses were the true litmus test that determined if my physical attraction was more than surface level. Once in junior high, this boy named Terry, in what I assume was his way of trying to impress me, threw me up against the wall in the stairwell (very dramatic, very *90210*) and frantically stuck his tongue in my mouth. It was obnoxiously wet with no direction or rhythm. We were dating, or doing as much "dating" as one does when they're in junior high. I don't think we liked one another all that much, but he was nice enough. Either way, after that kiss, I knew whatever we had was over. The terrible tongue encounter sealed the deal.

Fast-forward to my sophomore year in college when I dated an Alpha. He was about five-ten (an honorable six feet tall with Timbs on) and his eyes would randomly change from hazel to light green and he drove a black Mustang. He was a popular guy on campus, whereas I kept more of a low profile. So, when we began getting to know one another, I couldn't believe he actually knew who I was much less wanted to date me. We were together for about a year and a half and whenever we kissed it felt like it was just the two of us on the entire campus. One spring day before we decided to be exclusive, the sororities and fraternities were out on the yard. The Alpha and I walked hand-in-hand from his off-campus apartment and as we approached the university, I wiggled my hand out of his to wave goodbye and head back to my dorm. In private we acted boyfriend and girlfriend-y, but when we were in public, I knew enough not to expect that behavior since we weren't together for real. After my polite, very platonic, very church-y goodbye, he looked at me, bit his lip (a telltale sign something naughty crossed his mind), grabbed my waist, and kissed me in front of everyone. In my mind, I was like *OhMyGod! OhMyGod! OhMyGod! I just got signed to the record label.* Aside from the public declaration of our relationship, his kisses made me feel electric and desired and like he really liked *me.* That's what good kisses do. They silence the noise and they're a taste test for what's romantically to come. Stephen's kiss did that and more. Yes, it was pleasurable, but it also emotionally woke me up from my own comatose romantic state. I'd been working nonstop trying to make a name for myself as a writer, so I had totally neglected the idea of partnership. I didn't realize how long it had been since I'd liked a guy until I kissed Stephen. I didn't know how vast the romantic side of me was until that moment happened. There was a whole other aspect of Shenequa I hadn't explored and hadn't deemed important enough to investigate because being a "successful writer" took priority, and it wasn't until my romantic encounter with Stephen that I realized how much of me I was neglecting.

Back in the Uber, the driver pulled up to his hotel on the Lower East Side and let us out. We made small talk as he walked me to the train, but I didn't hear what he was saying. All I could think about was what happened on the ride over. There were a few low murmurs from people pissed at us for partially blocking the train entrance, but I didn't care. MTA doesn't respect anybody, so they were probably going to miss their train anyway. The light strawberry sky had turned a deep plum, and the faint breeze from earlier was now sharper. Stephen kissed me again, this time tilting my head upward to meet his six-foot-four frame.

"Text me when you get home, yeah?"

He kissed my forehead, my nose, and then my lips one last time before heading back to his hotel, and before he was out of sight, I tried my hardest to hide my giddy smile. As I searched for my MetroCard, I realized now I was going to miss my train, but in all my euphoria, I didn't care. I was on cloud nine, ten, and eleven! I felt great! Amazing! Full of life! I felt that rush of excitement you experience whenever the little buzzer thingy they give you at The Cheesecake Factory finally lights up. I had been bold enough to ask a gorgeous man for a kiss and he had obliged. *I* was finally being "chosen" by a guy *I* wanted. But more importantly, the way Stephen's lips felt against mine proved to me that I wasn't hollow inside. I was more than the brick and mortar I half-assumed I'd become after years of no romance.

So, babe, if you've gotten this far in the chapter, congratulations! However, I suggest you buckle your seatbelt because we're going to take a sharp left. No, I'm not going to inundate you with calls about your car's extended warranty. Instead, we're now about to enter what I like to call the *Oh, you thought* portion of the story.

There are several ways to let someone know you're not interested, or as the youth once called it "to curve someone." It can happen with an unreturned phone call, or a text message left on read. If you've met someone with actual home training, manners, or empathy, then this curve may come via an honest conversation, albeit an uncomfortable one. Those curves still hurt, but they're the most respectful.

Then you have the "*I mean, you're cool but . . .*" kind of curve that's the hardest to detect in the beginning. They'll engage with you only after you initiate the conversation. They'll respond to your calls or text messages, but never help to carry the dialogue past the courteous yet unimaginative "My day was good. How about yours?"

The person will interact with you out of kindness, not desire.

The "*I mean, you're cool but . . .*" curve is made known in the hours it takes for them to respond to a text or phone call because you're only busy when you're not *that* interested. "I left my phone on the charger" or "I was in the other room" are all legitimate reasons why you might miss someone's call or text, but it's been my experience that when you're really into someone and they're into you, the calls and conversation are timely and consistent.

The "*I mean, you're cool but . . .*" curve can also be detected in how polite the person is when they speak with you. It's a fine line, yes. You don't want to be disrespectful and offend someone, but jokes, warmth, and laughter often live outside of the "Yes, please" and "Thank you for asking" boundary line. Formality slowly falls by the wayside and compassionate comfortability, along with jokes, takes over.

The "*I mean, you're cool but . . .*" curve is a bit more original than the "*Damn, I didn't see this message*" curve because we're frankly more concerned with our phones than the mounting out-of-network payments we owe our therapists, so please.

The "*I mean, you're cool but . . .*" curve is probably done with good intentions. It's not that the person doesn't like you; it's just they don't *like you* like you.

Anyone and everyone gets curved.

At first, I thought Stephen and I were on the same page. Before our date we once spent an hour on the phone talking about a bunch of useless things, like why *The Lion King* is the best Disney film of all time, and how *Zootopia* should be used in all corporate D.E.I. training seminars. He gave a ten-minute dissertation on his respect and admiration for Frank Ocean ("His lyrics are too mysterious for me. I don't know if he's talking about a past lover or his pet goat that died," I said), and I followed up with why *The Golden Girls* may be one of the few entities in America that surpass race. He told me about his family, skydiving, his travels, and that one time he spent seventy-five dollars on a room-service steak. I talked about my mom, my journeys throughout Europe, all the people I've in-terviewed as a former entertainment reporter, and the meaning behind my ten tattoos. (There's no deep meaning, y'all. It was mostly me being in my twenties.) It was, from my estimation, a great conversation.

But then he had to go back on the road. Stephen's a musi-cian, so he travels. I should've mentioned this before—that and the fact that he's younger than me. I wanted to put off the deep, Black woman sigh, accompanied with an eye roll and accented by the ever-so-appropriate "Girl, you really tried it! Why are you just now mentioning this?"

For months I held onto that kiss, our conversations, and what I thought was a connection. I knew things were bad once I noticed how validated I felt if he liked one of my photos or viewed one of my stories on social. Three hundred people could like a picture I posted (which is a personal high), but the minute Stephen liked it, that's when I felt seen, that's when it mattered. Growing annoyed from not knowing for certain if I was the only one who felt something, I sent him an email.

For weeks I've been trying to decide if I should send this email and was at a loss for words while writing it, which is a humbling feeling for a writer.

I don't know how to say it, so I guess I'll just say it: I like you. I like you a lot. Yes, you're beautiful and yes, you're talented, but there was an unexpected fluidity between us during our initial encounter that surprised me because I am, admittedly, a very staccato kind of woman. I trusted the feeling because it's not one I experience often. I believe as people we should name our beasts—good, bad, or indifferent—and that feeling I have been salivating over for such a long time was, simply, connection.

For the last four months, I've been replaying in my mind the kiss we shared. For me, it was an awakening. It was proof the lights still work and that I'm not dead on the inside. That kiss was refreshing, welcoming, and exciting all at the same time.

You've always been receptive, respectful, and kind whenever I've contacted you. I've never once felt as if you saw a message from me and rolled your eyes in annoyance. Over time, however, a feeling of doubt began

*to emerge because while you've always responded
to my messages, you never initiated dialogue.*

*You don't owe me anything. You don't owe me a call
when you're in town, nor do you owe me any explanation.
You're a busy musician establishing yourself. I get it.
While I am not in your industry per se, our industries
do cross paths, so I understand how hectic things
get. Maybe I wrongly assumed feelings were mutual.
I just kind of hoped that our kiss and subsequent
conversations would've inspired more reciprocity.*

*If you want to respond to this email, I'm more than willing
to hear your side of the story. If not, that's cool too.*

With love, kindness, and ferocious honesty.[1]

I didn't hear a peep for about a week. He confirmed he received the email in a brief text, but that's all. As a writer, my words are my weapons, but while drafting this message I second-guessed everything. Before sending the email, I had Grace and Ashleigh, who are also writers, look it over.

Should I say this?

Maybe I should take this part out?

Am I missing a comma in this sentence?

What's a good way to say "I really like you and I felt something, so please don't break my heart?"

After keeping my cool and being patient, I couldn't handle it anymore. So, I called.

"Good evening."

"Hello," he replied. "How are you? Everything cool?"

Before we got into the thick of the conversation, I could feel the rejection wrapped inside a holiday gift box of politeness ready to be unwrapped. No matter how many times someone says no to you, it still hurts, and I could smell that this was going to be one of those times.

"So yeah, the email," he said. "It's a lose-lose situation for me because, and please correct me if I'm wrong, but I didn't know you felt that way. I just thought you were trying to get some dick. In your email you spoke about connection. You put yourself out there. If I knew that's how you felt, I would have behaved differently."

Trying. To get. Some. Dick?

The words echoed in my head as Stephen continued explaining himself. I let out a nervous laugh because that's all I could do at the moment. When it mattered most to speak up and say something, I laughed. I laughed to protect myself from the boulder of disappointment that was Ubering its way from my gut to my heart. I laughed because laughing felt like a closer reaction to logic than the real sadness I was feeling. I laughed to make *him* feel comfortable because at *that* moment his comfort meant more than my shame. If he couldn't handle my romantic feelings for him, he certainly couldn't handle the embarrassment I felt being rejected by him. Better for us to laugh together than for me to cry alone.

He went on and on about him not knowing I felt this way and after a while I tuned him out. I don't remember how we ended the conversation, but I do remember suppressing a lump of tears in my throat and trying my best to not let him hear my sniffles or the crack in my voice. I'm an adult. I should be able to deal with rejection. The first man to deny me was my father (more on this later), so Stephen should've been a walk in the park. Easy-peasy lemon squeezy, as they say.

But it wasn't. It really wasn't.

After Stephen revealed he was clueless about my feelings for him, I was beside myself. In my mind it made no sense why he wouldn't want to date me, which only fueled a deeper confusion. I'm cute and fly, he's cute and fly. Why weren't we together? But my puzzlement was really ego, and once that subsided, I realized the uncertainty was less about Stephen's dumbass not wanting me and more about why it's so hard to get the guy I really want. If I roll back the surveillance footage of my dating experiences, a lot of times I've settled for a guy who was good, but not exciting, which is the male equivalent of a mushy apple. Mushy apples aren't the worst things in the world. They're still apples, rich in fiber and all that jazz, but, like, who wants a mushy apple? My dating experiences have either been he's cute, but he's broke, or he's not broke, but he's medium cute, or he's cute, he has a job, but he thinks it's okay to call the mother of his twin girls a cunt (true story). Finding a "crisp apple," or a man who's emotionally intelligent; financially stable; attractive; not homophobic, transphobic, misogynistic; funny, smart, and not profoundly insecure can feel like a fool's errand. It felt like Stephen had those things, so to be denied by Stephen also felt like I was being denied the qualities in a man I valued.

In the weeks after our call, I kept quiet about everything. Grace and Ashleigh were going through their own mess with their respective guys, and I was still processing the whole *trying to get some dick* fallout. For months I longed for more of him only to realize that I wasn't even a factor to him. I dreamed about us in the Uber only to then learn I was holding onto something he let go of probably as soon as he shut the car door. I tried watering down my feelings and being an adult about the matter (which is hella overrated by the way). I wanted whatever part of him he would allow me to have, so I tried being an associate. I quickly realized that wouldn't work. I had it bad for this guy and friendship alone wouldn't suffice. Yes, I wanted to get to know him better—his likes, dislikes, his quirks, and sense of humor—but I wanted all of that under a romantic umbrella.

Maybe I had hoped for too much too soon. Or maybe he couldn't pick up on the breadcrumbs I left. Maybe I should go around kissing other guys in Ubers so next time all I'll get is gingivitis and not get so attached. (Can you get gingivitis from kissing? Is that a thing?) Maybe I needed to get a grip, get over it, and not waste any more time on a guy who doesn't like me. I could drown in all the maybes.

Shows like *Living Single*, *Sex and the City*, or even *A Different World* made dating seem like it happened weekly. There was always a cute guy who would pop up at a nearby bookstore or coffee shop. You'd glance, he'd make eye contact, approach you, and then boom! A first date would happen. In the real world, or at least in my world, that was not the case. Once I became of age to really explore dating, men weren't making eye contact. They weren't initiating conversation. They weren't approaching. So, those organic first meetings that led to flirty first dates I saw on television simply weren't happening, which made Stephen seem like a unicorn.

Another factor that contributed to my lackluster dating life was my upbringing. I was raised by a fierce group of Jamaican women who had all their children before the age of twenty-one and raised them, unfortunately, with little or no help from the father. So, instead of being given the room to appropriately date as a tween and then receive more freedom as I got older, I was told to keep my nose in my books. Why? Well, it was believed that your education can't hurt you, but dating can, hence why I went full steam ahead in my career. Boys are dumb, men are

dumber, so best work toward achieving some semblance of sta-
bility because the male species will mess all that up. And while
my mother's and aunts' experiences are valid, there is something to be said about learning who you are through a romantic
lens. Had I been able to date here and there, maybe Stephen's
kiss could've rolled off my back sooner instead of clinging to
me the way it did. Dating, sex, romance, situationships, they
all build muscles and expose you to you in a way that an A+ or
a new job or a promotion can't.

Rejection from someone you fancy also does that.

Listen, everybody experiences it, whether it's that you
didn't get into the college you wanted or that dream job you
interviewed for. People hear the word "no" all the time, but a
professional rejection doesn't sting as much as a romantic one.
Getting a certain gig waters your self-worth in a weird way. As
much as we like to front and say we're not our careers, a lot of
us, most of us (myself included), don't know how to separate
who we are from what we do. My dear friend Salaam was the
first person to ever point this out to me. He's an incredibly successful musician and producer and has worked with some of my
favorite artists, but if you ask him about himself, he leads with
his personhood and not his profession.

Romantically, when someone rejects you, it stings and then
cuts below the epidermis of it all. When Stephen so eloquently
reduced my robust feelings for him to a romp in the hay, it
felt like an indictment on my worth. According to the book
The Four Agreements, which my friend Nic has been trying to
get me to read since 2011, you're not supposed to take things
personally, but, like, how? (Maybe I would know if I read the
book.) Senior year of high school I asked a guy to go to the
prom with me and he said no. I went out on a limb and asked a
guy and still got curved! I ended up going by myself, but it was

still kind of crummy because the person I wanted didn't want me. How is a no, in the romantic context, directed at me not supposed to be taken deeply?

I finally told Grace and Ashleigh about Stephen, and they were supportive. As much as society tells us that men are simple, I actually think they're just as complicated and as emotional as women. Ashleigh, however, was of a different mindset.

"Dudes really be black and white most times," she said. "Either they like you or they don't."

I didn't respond to Ashleigh's comment, but I knew I didn't agree. Yes, it stinks when you like a guy and they don't like you, but simply reducing like to black or white, left or right, on or off reduces, in my opinion, the vast spectrum of like. I not only love coffee, but I really, really like it (more on this in subsequent chapters). I do not want to live a life in which I wake up and I do not have coffee. I would rather be stripped of my tastebuds than not enjoy a cup of Joe. I also like blueberries. I dig 'em. I think they're pretty cool in how they help fight against Alzheimer's allegedly, but do I like blueberries in everything? No. I think a man can like you but not like you-like you. I think a man can be gung ho about you and then after a conversation or two decide she's dope, but she's not for me. I think a man can like things about you but not enough to enter into a full-fledged relationship with you. The idea of liking someone has various degrees and levels, and not everyone, not even a cutie patootie writer from Queens with a quirky sense of humor, makes the final cut all the time.

Stephen's rejection also made me question how I might be perceived. Are cute guys actually insecure? Do Mushy Apple men have nothing to lose? Is this all just a numbers game? Maybe it's a confidence thing? Maybe I don't evoke as much strength as I should to attract better men? I could've sworn I had a Leo moon. There are some women who seem to always have a Michael B. Jordan or Damson Idris type of guy on their arm, and I sincerely can't relate. First of all, where are you even meeting these men? Home Depot? And what are you doing to get them to (A) notice you; (B) ask for your number; (C) call; and (D) follow up with an actual planned date?

To say I experienced growth after everything would be too grand a statement and not entirely accurate. I acknowledged that Stephen didn't feel the same and the hurt eventually dissipated in the same way the pain of biting your tongue eventually goes away on its own. It's real. It hurts like all get out, but sooner or later it dies. I didn't turn my pain into purpose. I didn't launch a successful nonprofit organization for rejected women either. I think I just accepted the emptiness. This faux healing was disrupted from time to time when my never-ending need for an answer that made more sense returned. "What did I do wrong?" I'd question. I'd replay, fast-forward, and edit everything that occurred between us with the hope that if I had done one thing differently maybe I would've gotten the boy I wanted. All those mental gymnastics were futile. I would've been more successful trying to eat a pair of jeans.

At the end of the day, it boils down to this simple fact: I liked a boy, and he didn't like me back, and that sucked. It really, really sucked, but it be's like that sometimes, ya know?

5

Two Sugars with Hazelnut Cream

Content Warning:
This chapter contains references to sexual assault and rape.

I've never told anyone this, but most nights I go to bed excited about the cup of coffee I'll drink in the morning. It's not a jump for joy kind of excitement, or an exaggerated *yesssss* followed by an aggressive hand gesture either. It's more of a gentle tickle that turns into an internal warm smile. Some nights I read before bed, other nights I mindlessly scroll through social media, but before I close my eyes, I think about my fingers hugging my favorite mug as I sip the warm cup of coffee that I'll have in eight or ten hours, and then I'm happy.

I don't remember when coffee first slow-dripped its way into my orbit. It might've been sometime after college, but now it's become a permanent fixture in my life. Getting out of bed isn't a chore per se, but it damn sure isn't as easy as it was when I was in my twenties, so yes, coffee is also a tool used to wake me up and get me going. Things changed for the better after I discovered coffee creamers, in particular hazelnut coffee creamer. The addition of the smooth and sweet cream mixed in

with the bitter jolt of energy from the coffee gives me a necessary balance. Throw in two sugars and I have reached nirvana.
The cream must be hazelnut, not half-and-half, or skim, or the
Birkin bag of the creamer world, oat milk. My order is specific,
enjoyable, and it never leaves me needing or wanting more.

Once faced with an unexpected, wicked case of heartburn,
my doctor suggested giving up coffee for a while. I told him I'd
rather hug a cactus. The idea of sacrificing something so use-
ful and pleasurable sounded asinine. Yes, at the time, the dark
roast I was drinking was too strong, but saying no to all coffee
wasn't something I was or am willing to do.

I can give up sex. I cannot give up coffee.

That might sound extreme to some, but for me, coffee has a
higher satisfactory rate than sex. As I round out my first year
of abstinence, I can honestly say I don't miss sex that much.
Unfortunately, I'm a heterosexual woman and having sex with
men can sometimes (oftentimes) not be that great. According
to a 2017 study published in the *Archives of Sexual Behavior*,
52,588 adults were surveyed and of the straight women who
participated, they reported having an orgasm about 65 percent
of the time, compared with lesbians, who said they experienced
orgasms about 86 percent of the time.[1]

Like I said, statistically speaking, having sex with men can
be . . . lackluster.

There are too many variables that have to occur for sex to be
an enjoyable experience for me. Penis size, for one, plays a huge
role (pun intended) and how much foreplay, if any, is another.
For coffee, I've figured out what works and I don't have to devi-
ate much from that. If I want to add a little razzle-dazzle to the
equation, I can switch up the creamer. International Delight
had a birthday cake flavor that hit the spot, but it's been discon-
tinued because the brand clearly enjoys chaos. So yeah, I can

get adventurous when it comes to my cup of Joe if I want to. Getting adventurous when it comes to sex on the other hand can be a crapshoot.

A friend of mine who refuses to say "good morning"—he once offered: "How about I say, 'Welcome to 11:39' as a middle ground?"—said new sex is exciting, but old sex is trustworthy, which is a fair and accurate assessment. The thrills that come with being intimate with someone new include, but are not limited to:

Sexy Talk

When you and your partner have decided sex is on the horizon, both parties often partake in a bit of sexy talk/flirtation to generate excitement about the forthcoming romp. Whether it be subtle or over-the-top, putting into words what will later take place ignites the imagination, breaks up the monotony of the day, and helps you tune out Scott from sales when he tries to pitch you KFC's new four-dollar chicken sandwich (true story). Whether it's how good you allegedly are on top, or how he can make love until the break of dawn like all '90s R&B singers alleged, hyping up the moment adds to the exhilaration of new sex.

Seeing the Other Person Naked for the First Time

Chances are you've seen a naked person several times before you and your new partner get naked, but the anticipation that sexy talk builds finally comes to a head when they take off their clothes. Bodies come in all kinds of varieties. Some of us are curvy, some have well-toned physiques, and lots of us are built like an IKEA bookcase. But when we're finally naked in front of the other person, no one is getting all wide-eyed over an elbow or someone's clavicle. It's the roundness of a woman's bum, the muscles that bulge in a man's biceps. It's the breasts, thighs, lips, and the magic between someone's legs that most of us lust after. Seeing that up close makes the wait—however long or brief—worth it.

Actually Having Sex with the New Person

The physical pleasures of sex can't be duplicated and its why so many people really *really* love it and will risk their careers, marriages, and lives for it. No other experience comes close. Having a Monday off from work is cool, but it's not sex. Finding a twenty-dollar bill in your winter jacket is cool, but it's not sex. Receiving a tracking number for your new Williams-Sonoma nonstick skillet is pretty dope, but for a lot of people, it won't and can't compare to sex. So, when you combine sexy talk, seeing your partner naked for the first time, and then experiencing seventeen-ish minutes of the highest form of physical pleasure humans share with another person, you can understand why new sex is the bees-knees for so many people.

Old sex, however, also has its perks. Old sex, or sex with someone familiar, doesn't have to be sexy, fancy, or dramatic. Old sex can mean you and your partner have figured out what works for both of you so you can count on a good time. Old sex is also comfortable, like your favorite pair of sweats. It can be fun and even a little silly, which takes away the pressure of having to demonstrate whatever expertise you've acquired throughout the years. It's reliable like a peanut butter and jelly sandwich. Maybe someone falls off the bed, or a fart escapes from Alcatraz, not the silent farts that are as deadly as a white cop who "feared for his life." I'm talking about the loud ones, which aren't so bad. Old sex can be good sex devoid of the "performance factor" that comes with new sex. New sex is the cute restaurant that opened; old sex is Uber Eats (no delivery fee) and a *Law & Order: SVU* marathon featuring episodes with B. D. Wong.

But whether it's old sex, new sex, or casual sex, I still prefer coffee. I'm aware some will think I'm insane. Even fellow coffee lovers might shake their head in astonishment that I would go so far as to compare the exquisite taste and reliability of coffee to the physical enjoyment of sex, but for me, it all boils down to trust. I can trust coffee will do the job 90 percent of the time. I trust coffee has just as much respect for me as I do for it. Coffee never pinned me down on a couch and forced me to spread my legs like James did.

I was in my late twenties when we met one night in Times Square. I was with a few friends from work when James caught my eye. He was tall-ish and well dressed. It wasn't love at first sight but he seemed fun, and I decided why not? We exchanged numbers and agreed to go to lunch a few days later. For our date, I wore a black turtleneck and jeans and thought I was doing something fancy with a dash of mascara and two-dollar black eyeliner I purchased from the nearby Queens Village beauty supply store.

"You like Caribbean food?" he asked as I buckled my seatbelt in his car.

"What type of question is that? Of course, I like Caribbean food. Isn't everyone from New York half West Indian almost?"

"You right. You right," he said as he pulled off.

What I assumed would be a quaint sit-down eatery for us to get to know one another turned out to be a busy takeout restaurant. The loud flat-screen television showing a soccer game made it almost impossible to hear the cashier call out ticket numbers for customers whose food was ready. The wind chime hanging above the door rang incessantly as patrons walked in and out of the cramped location. "Coming through! Hot pan! Hot pan!" a man shouted as he rushed from out the back to behind the counter to refill an almost empty tray of curry shrimp. Impatient customers stood against a wall or sat on the railing where flyers of bikini-clad buxom brown women promoting a boat ride party with "special guest" Beres Hammond collected dust.

As I looked around at what appeared to be choreographed chaos, I became irate. I put on eyeliner for this "date" only to be brought to a hole-in-the-wall that didn't even have seats.

"I always get the brown stew chicken with rice and peas," James said. "What you want?"

I wanted to go home.

I was annoyed I even spritzed Chanel perfume on my neck and behind my ears to be here. In my book, first dates don't happen at to-go spots. They happen at a restaurant or maybe a bowling alley, someplace public where an activity can happen, like at the game night where we met. I didn't know that for James, the word "date" was code for "grab some food and bring it back to my couch in my living room." What I also didn't know how to do at the time was speak up. I was conflicted. There was a part of me that was afraid I would ruin the mood if I asked him to take me home. I didn't want to be labeled a "gold digger" because he bought me food, which was such an asinine thing to think in retrospect, but it's the truth. His lack of effort was such a turnoff, but I knew he didn't see it that way. Yet, if I vocalized how over it I was, he could've gotten pissed and left me stranded on the other side of Queens, forcing me to take a dollar cab and two buses just to get back home. Queens is weird in that regard. A place or an event could be fifteen minutes away by car and then forty-days-and-forty-nights away via public transportation. There was also a teeny-tiny part of me that still wanted the date to work because I wanted to have a nice date with a guy. All of these factors went through my head as I stood against a wall waiting for my jerk chicken, so instead of speaking up I just . . . waited for my jerk chicken.

Once we got the food, we went to his place and settled on the couch to eat. Then it happened. And it happened quickly. One minute we were eating and watching TV, the next I was trying my best to push him off me, angry he was on top of me but angrier at myself that I wasn't strong enough to get him off of me. Yet, despite my efforts he persisted until he was fully inside of me. When it was done—when *he* was done, I pulled up my pants and he drove me home. And one of the cruelest acts of the entire day was the fact that he kissed me on the cheek as I removed my seat belt before exiting the car. A kiss so soft, so tender, it was the antithesis of his inhumane actions. He waited in his car until I was inside my apartment before he drove off.

"Hey, Chin," Mommy said sitting on the couch. "How was your day?"

"Fine, Mommy. It was fine," I said.

I've never had to lie to Mommy about how my coffee tasted or about my coffee in general because coffee has never hurt me. I've always known what I was getting into whenever I brewed a pot myself or bought some from one of the guys on the street who have those little coffee stands. I've kept my rape from my mom because how do you tell your mom you were raped? How do you even have that conversation? I wish I could say I'd never been sexually assaulted, let alone more than once. Unfortunately, that isn't my experience. The second time happened a few years later, maybe three or four, at the hands of an ex-boyfriend. And after he was done assaulting me, he attempted to soothe my rage with his own arrogance after violating me inside of a Midtown Manhattan hotel room.

"Where's the condom I gave you?" I said after penetrating me and I asked him to stop.

"Whoops," he said smiling. "I guess I must've lost it."

"Whoops!" I said, anger now rising.

Once he realized I wasn't entertained he immediately went on the defense, assuring me he was "healthy" and "clean."

"Do you know how much I love me?" he said. "Do you think I would put *myself* at risk? I get tested all the time."

Whew! Thank God for that, right? Because my ex assured me his health and cleanliness are so paramount to *him* it meant it was okay he didn't use a condom even though I gave him one to put on.

But what never dawned on my ex was maybe *I* wasn't healthy and clean. Maybe I didn't get tested all the time. In his selfish desire for control, it never crossed his mind that maybe the condom was my way of protecting him from something I didn't want to reveal. Something I've learned throughout my years of dating is that a lot of men do not factor in danger. It never crosses their mind that they could be hurting themselves. The power a lot of men feel to do whatever they want when it comes to women blinds them from the notion that they could be endangering themselves as well. My ex didn't know if I was up to date with my own STD screening, but that didn't matter because he wanted to use my body in the way *he* chose.

My ex reacted as if this was a schoolyard prank and not assault. Initially, I was furious! How dare he make an executive decision about *my* body! There was a time when I loved my ex. I shared laughs and dreams and spoke of a future with this man. How could he have done this? And then immediately, I felt small, so very small. He used my body to betray me and subsequently showed me that the agency I thought I had meant nothing if a man wanted access to it. James used brute strength, but my ex used the good times of our past with a healthy portion of deceit to hurt me. The shame was unbearable and suffocating. I wanted nothing to do with the shell or encasing that I was born with. I wanted out, but there was nowhere, emotionally or literally, for me to go. I checked my cell. It was two in the morning, and public transportation was iffy and taking a train that late at night all the way to Queens posed a whole new level of danger. This was before the convenience of Uber and Lyft, so I couldn't order one. Yellow cabs from the city to my house were pricy as all get out, and if I had twenty bucks in my wallet at the time, I considered myself rich. None of my friends had cars, so calling someone to come and get me was out of the picture as well. My only choice was to stay there until morning.

Lying in the bed with the man who assaulted me was a humiliation I couldn't shake but had to withstand. Surprisingly, though, I didn't cry. For the remaining four or five hours I dozed in and out of sleep, exhausted from the emotional and physical damage that had taken place but feeling not safe enough and too scared to actually allow myself to really rest. The next morning, I dressed, left his hotel room before he woke up, and took the train home.

"Hey, Chin!" Mommy asked when I walked in. "How'd it go? You two getting back together?"

"Nah, Mommy. We're definitely not getting back together," I said.

It would be years later, while watching Michaela Coel's transformative *I May Destroy You* that I learned what my ex did to me was similar to stealthing, which is the act of removing a condom during sex without the other person's knowledge. Watching Zain (played by Karan Gill) sneakily take off the condom while in bed with Coel's character, Arabella, affirmed that my anger was righteous and my ex's *Do you know how much I love me?* was selfish, woefully insensitive, and assault.

. . .

Every other month there's a news report alleging that if you drink two or more cups of coffee a day, you're going to die in thirty minutes with your big toe protruding from your forehead, and I am here to tell you, even if that were true, I still wouldn't stop drinking coffee. The reliability, predictability, and joy I feel when drinking coffee isn't something I will give up. Those three factors are just some of the qualities that bleed into my definition of safety and unfortunately that's not something I experience often with men, especially a lot of the guys I've slept with. I've had sex with men other than James and the ex, but I haven't always felt safe with men before having sex with them, which as I type this, is so very sad to admit. If any part of me didn't feel comfortable, safe, or even in the mood, then why did I have sex with these men? I'll tell you why: it's because I was young, it's because I wanted to be wanted, it's because I was unsure of how to advocate for myself, afraid of violent retaliation, fearful of being viewed as a tease, the list goes on and on.

All of my unfulfilled wants have left me exhausted and defeated. Coffee gives me energy and a boost. I've had the occasional bad cup and let me tell you, it sucks, but I've never felt cheated by a cup of coffee in the way I've felt cheated in my dating experiences. More importantly, there's the safety issue. Yeah, I might burn my tongue if my coffee is too hot, but in a lot of my dating experiences, some aspect of me, whether emotionally or physically, is in some sort of danger. Why should I continue to give myself to men with the *possibility* of getting what I want in return? If I drink coffee seven days a week, five of those days I have a good cup. Those are pretty good odds, no?

Twice my body has been used as a trash bin for someone else's pleasure. And the times when I wasn't being sexually assaulted, I was dealing with the all-too-common yet still hurtful and manipulative games that often come with men who just want you for sex.

Once, I learned via social media the guy I was seeing conveniently decided to get back together with his ex-girlfriend mere hours after we had sex. What was the caption, again? "Reunited and it feels so good." Yeah, that was a tough pill to swallow at twenty-three years old. So, with so much emotional disenchantment that I've experienced sexually, my yearlong abstinence has proven to be one of the easiest and smartest sexual decisions I've ever made. Another unexpected bonus that came with not having sex is a clean and healthy vagina. As a woman, I've had the pleasure of experiencing several parties in my lady parts, including bacterial vaginosis, vaginitis, yeast infections, and all the other festivities that come when you have sex with a man who throws off your pH balance. The itch caused by BV is maddening, a brief reprieve experienced only when a stream of urine passes through. The infection made me balloon with frustration and fear. Surely, my vagina was about to fall off and roll into a nearby sewer, only to be fetched from the Hudson weeks later as evidence during an episode of *Law & Order: SVU* with special guest B. D. Wong.

When I went to Planned Parenthood, the gynecologist assured me this was common for sexually active women and promised me my vagina would be okay. My nerves simmered when she handed me a prescription for metronidazole and sent me on my way. I can't tell you how many times I've sat alone in a gynecologist's office, embarrassingly explaining my symptoms after having sex. Spreading my legs open for any one of the one-hundred-and-seventy men I'd been with—Kidding! I'm kidding, y'all (just wanted to see if you were still with me)— only to then place my feet in the stirrups in a cold doctor's office is humbling. I didn't have sex by myself, but I handled the responsibility of having sex by myself. All the men were conveniently busy. And the safe sex pamphlets in the waiting room do a great job of increasing your anxiety. One photo of a penis or vagina littered with warts and now your heart rate is sky high. It's also hella ironic that the week you're waiting for your STI results you see every pharmaceutical commercial featuring a happy-go-lucky white woman shopping, a middle-aged Black man trying yoga in the park, and a racially ambiguous person sitting on a bench holding a camera and they're all promoting the new drug that's "fighting back."

Don't let super gonorrhea take control! Fight back with vermecklicyde. Taken once daily, super-gonorrhea will lose its super status and Twitter verification and just become regular gonorrhea that won't ever go away. Side effects include headache, nausea, dizziness, shortness of breath, yellow toenails, your West Indian or West African mother forcing you to speak to a distant family member she video chatted during a blurry WhatsApp call, dandruff, and your ankle socks always sliding down the back of your heel no matter how many times you fix it. Fight back with vermecklicyde.

Even safe sex comes with its own set of challenges. During one vigorous romp with The Boy from East New York (the one who got me the Air Max 97s), the condom came off.

"Wait. Stop!" he said.

"What? What happened?" I replied breathless.

"You don't feel that?"

"Feel what?" I asked.

"The condom came off," he said, wiping beads of sweat from his forehead.

Looking down at his bare penis, I took a deep sigh. I rolled over onto my back and with his index and middle finger, The Boy from East New York gently fished out the remainder of the condom.

"Did it break?" I asked, the excitement fading and anxiety rolling in.

"Nah," he said, tucking the used condom within the wrapper it came from. "But you should probably take a Plan B pill just in case."

Nothing kills a vibe in the bedroom quicker than the idea of responsibility. The next day, I walked to my local Walgreens after ordering a Plan B emergency contraceptive pill online. It was early morning when I arrived and after explaining to the pharmacist behind the counter why I was there, he didn't even look me in the eye before shouting: "Your Plan B pill is up at the front register, ma'am!" The white guy behind the counter, a man I see often, also informed me and anyone within earshot that my prescription was ready.

To say I left Walgreens embarrassed is an understatement. The people who ring up my Goldfish crackers, my Always Ultra Thin maxi pads (with wings), and drugstore nail polish now knew I had sex and that I needed to ensure I didn't get pregnant because of it. I was also in the hole fifty dollars. How did I find myself in this position? I was also nervous about what side effects would befall me after taking the pill. Would I get nauseous? Would I be dizzy? How would this affect my next period? Supposedly, the Plan B pill doesn't work if you weigh more than one hundred and sixty pounds. So, not only do I have to prevent a pregnancy, but I'm being body-shamed as well.

All of these thoughts jogged through my head as I downed the pill and chugged a bottle of water. The pleasure from the sex didn't matter in that moment. And regardless of the fact that I had done it with another person, *I* was the one who bore the responsibility. Yeah, *we* had sex, but *I* had to take the pill and incur whatever physical consequences that came from that. Whenever a dude isn't around, my vagina is fine. Let a penis enter the picture and everything from a condom gone rogue to potentially having a yeast infection that takes on a cottage-cheese consistency in my panties can happen. And, like, seriously, who wants that? Only white people eat cottage cheese. You think I want cottage cheese—or white people—in my panties?

Sometimes I wish I were like *Sex and the City*'s Samantha Jones or her *Golden Girls* ancestor, Blanche Elizabeth Devereaux (funny enough, Blanche's initials spell bed). Played by Kim Cattrall and the OG, Rue McClanahan, respectively, both women were fearless in their desire for and pursuit of sex. When they wanted a man around, they found a man, and when they didn't, they were content. Blanche could get a little antsy every now and then, but for the most part she was good. Sex, to a certain degree, was transactional for them, and the emotional aspect wasn't something either woman really needed. Unlike Samantha, Blanche, and even some of my own friends, I haven't had mind-blowing sex. Maybe if I'd had it would change my mind about the whole thing. When I hear my friends or people talk about their wonderous sexual experiences, I can't latch on to anything in the conversation. I'm usually there with a blank look on my face eating a box of Wheat Thins, patiently waiting for the topic to weave itself into something more universal like the latest acquittal of a white cop caught doing something blatantly racist.

Along with not having great sex, I've also seen an uptick in hypersexuality. What I've noticed is being pretty or cute doesn't even qualify you for the Attractive Olympics anymore. Now, you must be sexy, and the idea of being sexy and exuding sexiness bleeds into how sexual you supposedly are, and this idea has become so exaggerated that it causes some of us (myself included at one point) to don a persona that isn't particularly true to who we are in totality. Yes, there are spaces in which healthy conversations about sex and one's love for sex are had. But it feels like if you don't have a high sex drive and you're vocal about not having a high sex drive, you're viewed as a weirdo. You know what I think is more interesting than wanting to bone all the time? Oreos being on sale. (They're hella expensive for no reason.) Sex has its place, being sexy has its place, but now it feels like if you're not vocal about how freaky and sexy you are all the time, then you're out of place. For a lot of people sex is *thee* best thing ever, but unfortunately, my experiences don't allow me to meet them there. If they did, I wouldn't have so much ammo to write this chapter.

Abstinence has provided me with a safety net that I didn't know I could use. My abstinence is fueled by me. This is *my* choice. This is what *I* want to do. I no longer care about what men think. A lot of my beliefs about relationships and dating were built around what I thought men wanted and what I believed I had to do to be the specific girl *that* man desired. If the guy I was dating wanted the sexy girl, I would spend way too much money buying matching bras and panties or wearing uncomfortable lace thongs. If the backpack rap dudes wanted a backpack rap girl, I'd put on that persona, once studying Kendrick Lamar's tongue-twisting lyrics to "Rigamortis," hoping

I would be impressive enough to be "claimed." None of my chameleon-like transformations gave me the intimacy or commitment I was looking for. I wanted the guys I dated to value me and that isn't what happened. I foolishly bought into the belief that when a man thinks you're the one then he automatically acts better. It was after interrogating that sexist school of thought closely enough that I realized it placed undue pressure on women to "behave correctly" in order to get a man to conduct himself better, when men should be treating all women, not just "the one," with kindness and respect.

Getting rejected, disrespected, or disregarded, or being treated as an afterthought, rubs you raw after a while. At some point, you begin to question if you're worth anything, much less love; at least that's what I did and sometimes still do. It's hard to be confident when a majority of your dating experiences leave you crying. I was expected to prove why I should be someone's girlfriend. And the grand prize? A healthy, fruitful relationship filled with laughter, love, trips to the Amalfi Coast, and an occasional Netflix binge? Girl, no; it's most likely crumbs and maybe a "Happy birthday to a real one" shout-out in his Instagram stories . . . not his main feed.

Obviously, my abstinence might make it more challenging for me to find Mr. Right, but frankly, I've done enough legwork and I'm tired. Taking sex off the table allows me to better weed out the nonsense from the guys who really may be interested in me. It's also not lost on me that some men will view my abstinence as a challenge to their own manhood and attempt to talk me out of my panties. Sir, I'm telling you right now, it won't work, so I suggest you go on about your day.

Wait, so, Shenequa, how long will you be abstinent?

Excellent question. Until I'm good and ready. There's no set date. Maybe I'll wait until marriage or maybe I'll wait until death. Who knows. I would like to think I'm making room for a real foundation, mutual respect, and trust. Right now, sexual pleasure is far from my mind. During a late '90s interview, singer-songwriter George Michael brilliantly said: "It's very hard to be proud of your own sexuality when it's not brought you any joy. Once it's associated with joy and love, it's easy to be proud of who you are."[2] I totally related to what he was saying even though I'm not a gay man or a famous musician. For me, there have been very few times when sex has been a joyous, loving, pleasurable, and respectful situation. I haven't completely lost all of my libido, but it's gone for a walk, and I'm not inclined to chase after it.

I want something fulfilling and tangible; something strong, yet delicate and sweet when I need it to be. I'm looking for something that will give me the needed boost whenever I'm feeling sluggish and lazy. I want something comforting, reliable, warm, and tasty.

It just so happens that what I want in a relationship is also how I take my coffee.

6

Camera Off

If you're like me, then your Monday mornings begin Sunday evening at about seven. At quarter to, the realization that the weekend is over sets in and at the top of the hour you begin reading those wretched unanswered emails as you mentally prepare for what's to come. If you wait until morning to tackle everything (and it is a tackle), you're behind, so to have a fighting chance at winning the day, Monday gets to colonize a few hours from Sunday. Think of Mondays as the United States or the Great Britain of the workweek. It's unfair, but the alternative is drowning in meetings, emails, and potentially more meetings that could've been emails. It's this mental jolt from the freedom and ease of the weekend that makes Mondays so detestable. But worse than being the beginning of another arduous workweek, they're also the start of our collective performances.

Whether you willingly or unwillingly subscribe to it, a lot of us become classically trained actors from nine in the morning on Monday to about five in the evening on Friday. Why? Because that's part of what it means to adult. Work isn't just about executing the task; it's also about looking happy while doing it. It's about presenting as appreciative to have been given loads more work despite sometimes not having the resources to finish what's already piling up. It's also about appearing thrilled to be there every day no matter what's going on in the world or your personal life. Going through a nasty divorce? Who cares, you've got a job to do. Just learned your homegirl slept with your dad and now is about to be your stepmom? Buck up, buddy, at least you killed it during that presentation! When it comes to being a working adult, your life outside isn't something that should affect you while you're inside the office, and effectively participating in that separation of church and state, if you will, is what the professionals call "professionalism." This compartmentalization of your humanity in an effort to do the job you were hired to do is achievable, but it comes at a cost.

Sometimes work can be a needed distraction from life's woes. That surprise text from an ex that sends you spiraling (should've just blocked the number), what you thought was a benign tweet that's now gone viral and the quote RTs are vicious, or news of a loved one's illness can quickly become consuming, and work can dilute the sting of it all. But to constantly leave such a large swath of yourself at the door before crossing the threshold into the office can start to weigh on you. And that weight is even heavier when you're Black.

In March of 2020, my company made the decision to begin remote work for its employees due to the fast-moving coronavirus. As a homebody, not having to commute to the office felt like a blessing. I could walk to my kitchen, make a fresh pot of coffee, and ease into my morning divorced from experiencing the crescendo and urgency of the city. Being at the office at nine or ten in the morning, only to have my first meeting start at noon, isn't a vibe. I could've gotten more sleep, maybe allowed the lash glue to get a little tackier so the falsies could stay on, or simply not risked spraining my ankle while running down a flight of concrete stairs trying to catch the train. Working from home meant that I could reclaim more of my life, be more human, and not have to submit to the rigid demands and performances of work.

But then George Floyd was killed, brutally and in broad daylight, and just like that, the joy and, most importantly, the relaxation of remote work meant nothing. Former Minnesota police officer Derek Chauvin kept his knee on Floyd's neck for a little more than nine minutes and that murder, captured by a then teenage Darnella Frazier, shook up the world. What happened next were protests, racial tensions bubbling over, weird black boxes on social media showcasing solidarity, and Nancy Pelosi, along with other members of Congress, donning dashiki scarves and kneeling. It was . . . a lot and in such a short span of time. I felt like instead of giving the Black community the space to feel the feeling, the world knew something bad had happened and, instead, wanted to speed up the healing process. And when I say healing, I don't mean it in a therapeutic, let's-talk-this-out kind of way. I mean, someone grabbed the rubbing alcohol from the medicine cabinet and a few Band-Aids with little hearts on them and thought that simple patchwork job should've been enough. But it wasn't anywhere near enough, and because I felt so rushed, I also felt like I wasn't *allowed* to process any of it, and I damn sure couldn't emote during the workday. At the end of business, sure, I could close my laptop and cry, yell, scream, shout, let off some angry tweets, and let that be that. If that strategy didn't work, I'd grab my medical mask and take a walk around the block just to clear all the clutter in my head, and on the really rough days, I'd take several walks around the block. But these ripe feelings weren't relegated to the end of the business day. They weren't emails I could ignore or keynote presentations I could throw in my work computer trash bin. They were real and sticky! Sometimes they'd pop up on my way to the kitchen to get my second cup of coffee or during a meeting with a few white colleagues who seemed to have a bit too much ease about them. If I could sense or feel that there wasn't any concern, sadness, or even awareness of the global situation, I'd get pissed! How can you not bear any emotional weight in this situation? How dare you just be . . . okay?! Had I been in the office, there'd be nowhere for me to go and hide this anger, but with remote work a new hiding place unintentionally emerged.

I'm aware not every Black American had the luxury of switching to remote work. A lot of people still had to commute to a job and in doing so, they put their health in jeopardy during a time when little information was available about a deadly virus. Every day, people were dying by the boatloads. America's healthcare system quickly hit capacity, and so having to leave your home just to make ends meet took on a whole new meaning and danger. The pandemic didn't change everyone's lives or routines, and for those who still had to show up to work, their performances continued through heart-wrenching circumstances. Fortunately, this wasn't my experience.

The only way companies and employees were able to stay afloat, have meetings, and get work done was by way of videoconferencing tools. Zoom, Google Meet, and the weird one, Microsoft Teams, were what so many of us used to get through the day. For me, however, I took advantage of being in meetings without being seen. By turning my camera off and being on mute, I could let whatever emotion I had bottled up inside of me out. Did it solve all the problems related to the pandemic and the death of George Floyd? No, of course not, but it gave me more breathing room and it didn't force me to swallow my humanity in the name of "professionalism." As a

Black woman working in a corporate space, I've learned how to vocally camouflage (aka code switch) my normal human emotions that, when expressed, can be deemed "aggressive." So, I add a pinch of glee, diluting my annoyance when someone cuts me off, or I take a deep breath and speak in a calm tone despite the cayenne that's being thrown at me. These are all ways I've learned how to navigate and survive mostly white work environments. I have not, however, perfected this skill when it comes to my facial expressions. Several of my fellow Black colleagues have messaged me on the side while in meetings about the story I was telling just with my face alone: "*Yo, fix ya face!*" Whether it be a narrowing of my eyes if something nonsensical was said, a raised eyebrow and a head tilt if something questionable was spoken, or a full-on eye roll if some foolery occurred. My professionalism can be real shakey-bakey largely depending on what I hear. In the days and weeks after George Floyd's murder, I was not in the mood to perform the role of the good employee. I couldn't leave my feelings at the front door in the name of "professionalism."

So, behind the camera I hid.

Behind the camera I cried.

Behind the camera I fetched tissues, blew my nose, cleared my throat, unmuted myself and responded, "Sounds good!" or "I'm aligned," just to ensure I at least sounded present during meetings I didn't give a rat's behind about. In the first few days following Floyd's murder, I simply did not care. I didn't care about my job. I didn't care about deadlines. I didn't care about anything I was paid to care about, because if a Black man can be viciously killed in the middle of the day in front of a "live studio audience" if you will, then none of this really matters. Not this deck, not this presentation, not these clients, none of it. When I turned my camera off, I was allowed to sit in those feelings of anger and apathy. I was full of rage because here I was *again*, hurting and crying *again* due to the unjustified death of Black folks, and numb because it was two or three in the afternoon during the workweek, and I had to look alive and care about this dumbass job, because if I don't then these dumbass bills don't get paid.

Exhausted by it all, I wrote "Maintaining Professionalism in the Age of Black Death Is . . . a Lot" in May of 2020. My original title was going to be "I'm Tired of Being Nice to White People," but I decided against that headline and vibe. I penned this essay because I was over it, and as much frustration as I had inside of me, I also felt like the sympathy my people needed at the time was getting lost in rushing to heal, or in conversations about whether or not charges would be brought against Chauvin, as well as all the media coverage surrounding Floyd's death and subsequent protests. Debates about Floyd's past, the corruption within the police department, how brave Darnella Frazier was to record Floyd's final moments, juxtaposed against the cowardice of the other three cops who did nothing to help Floyd, were all stories being reported and conversations being had. But it felt like comforting a community, which had experienced such grotesque brutality, wasn't even a thought. I needed my colleagues and higher-ups to know that I and maybe other Black employees weren't okay. There's this popular saying: "It's okay to not be okay" and that's a lie. If that were true, then there would be a surplus of resources put in place, not just for those who aren't okay but for others to help those who aren't doing well. People would have the time and space to feel that concerning feeling, investigate where it came from, and work toward not just being okay but being better. Frankly, there aren't enough resources. If you're not okay, the quickest solution is calling in sick, praying your therapist can squeeze in an emergency session (and that's if you have insurance or enough money to cover the cost of therapy), or, if all else fails, walk over to your nearest Happy Hour to indulge in watered-down drinks.

I didn't write my essay because there hadn't been enough literature in regard to police violence. I wrote my story because I was hurt and sad and scared, and I needed my bosses to know why my work, especially in those first few weeks after Floyd's death, may not have been up to par. There was no time or space for those in-between feelings in the workplace. Joy is welcome, humor to a degree is okay, but anger, fear, uncertainty, confusion? There isn't enough money in the budget for those feelings. So, the idea of being empathetic isn't really a thing. Hell, even being polite can be viewed as a little odd. You're there to work, or that's the mentality, and any time spent being humane can be considered a waste. I can't tell you how many times colleagues throughout my career have jumped right into an ask and not even said "good morning." I could be walking into the office, coffee in hand with my coat still on, and here goes Steve from marketing asking about copy for the new campaign. The fact that I was being flooded with pictures of Chauvin's smug face with George Floyd's helpless and lifeless body underneath his knee didn't factor in for some folks, and if that wasn't registering, then my "slow to respond" approach to work assignments probably wasn't even factored in.

I didn't care about the client call.

I didn't care about the brainstorm.

I didn't care about the deadline.

I wrote directly from my heart, and I think it touched other people's hearts. I wasn't trying to be fancy. I wasn't trying to show off my impressive vocabulary. I simply wanted people to know how hurt I was, and it wasn't until I penned my story that it dawned on some of those outside of the Black community who read it that a death had actually occurred. A man lost his life, and I, along with many other Black people, were once again faced with trying to shake off the fear that we could be next, while also juggling anger, sadness, and hopelessness. I didn't think many people would read my essay. It felt as though every American news outlet was doing *another* deep dive examining police brutality and lawmakers' refusal to hold cops account-able for their actions. So, with the belief no one was paying me any attention, I wrote from a place of yearning. I wanted grace and softness to be extended while I and so many others traversed this all too familiar plane of Black death. I wanted all those in the C-suite to reconsider the long-held definition of professionalism and to cut me and my people a little slack. I needed tenderness. And so I poured all those wants and hopes into an essay, fully prepared for it to get lost within the sea of think pieces. I didn't think it would become one of the most talked-about pieces during that time. Turns out, when you get Jeff Bezos's attention, other people pay attention. (Who knew?) When he shared it on his Instagram feed, Billionaire Bezos gave my words some height. With his influence, my essay be-came a twenty-foot-tall lion, and CEOs, COOs, and every other executive with a title that can be dwindled down to an acronym listened.

I still don't know how Jeff Bezos saw my story. I reposted it a few times on Twitter, but how it moved so far up the chain is anyone's guess. I'm appreciative it did, because with Bezos's reshare and impact it reminded people that Black folks are hu-man. And as strong, beautiful, brilliant, creative, joyful, hilar-ious, and resilient as we are, unjustified Black death will never be normal. It's become normalized, yeah, but it's not *normal*. We've been and will continue to be skin, bone, and melanin.

In full transparency, I still don't know if other business leaders were listening to me, Shenequa, or if they were listening to the rich, white guy who told them to listen to Shenequa. There's a difference. Either way, some Black employees in corporate spaces now had a leg to stand on. If my words echoed how they felt, but they were too nervous to speak to their manager, then the easiest solve was, "I noticed Jeff Bezos reposted this essay on his Instagram account," and voila! You now had their attention.

Friends and associates in my industry reached out via DM or text to tell me my essay had made it a little bit easier for them to have tough conversations with their managers and supervisors. Discussions about empathy along with addressing the lack of diversity in some of their companies' departments were now on the table and I'm thankful. But I want to spend a little time here. Many Black employees were managing the enormous emotions that followed George Floyd's death and, yet, still found the courage to walk into their bosses' offices to talk about his death and their companies' office politics. That was no easy task. In the thick of all that grief, Black folks started worthwhile dialogue about race within the workplace that may have led to some change.

I had been at my gig for about a year when I wrote my essay, and I was happy my words had made a positive contribution for some Black employees. But, as I write this, more than three years after the start of the pandemic, and about two years after Chauvin was convicted, I'm beginning to realize the task of maintaining professionalism in the age of Black death was just the beginning.

In June 2022, the Supreme Group Chat overturned *Roe v. Wade*, leaving abortion rights up to the states and, in some extreme cases, not making an exception for rape, incest, or (dare I say it) if someone doesn't *want* to have a child but does want to enjoy the pleasures of sex. Books that don't center white cisgender folks or that honestly detail life for other communities were banned from schools, while shootings in schools, in grocery stores, at parades, and everywhere else people gather en masse took place across the country. These instances and many more proved to me that it isn't just Black death that requires you to dig deep and "remain professional." Life in general, especially in America, requires this performance from you as well. There is no safe space, no matter how much you try and cultivate one, which is why remote work, for me, is about more than just working from home.

Not having to fight my way onto public transportation was the first blessing that came with my new work life. Starting my morning at a slower pace has done wonders for my work productivity. On the days when everything is overwhelmingly busy, doing a load of laundry, washing the dishes, or even sweeping has become a way for me to de-stress while also staying on top of chores that would otherwise be left for the weekend. I'm one of those people who not only enjoys a clean house but also enjoys cleaning. Folding laundry has always felt like getting new school clothes and mopping or wiping down countertops puts me in a serene mood. Order and tidiness, especially in the home, keep me grounded when the world offers up another unprecedented event. (I inherited a handheld steamer weeks before Vladimir Putin's Russian soldiers invaded Ukraine, so that's been helpful.)

Remote work also allows me to take needed breaks throughout the day. Being expected to barrel through an eight-hour workday, respond to emails and Slack messages, ideate during brainstorms, and have enough brain power to actually execute whatever task needs to be executed is a lot to ask. In fact, it's not sustainable and it's what leads to burnout. Giving 1,000 percent every day isn't something I can do. My mood and will power fluctuate too much. I can easily toggle between "Aigh't, let's do this!" to "Aigh't, let's get this over with" in a span of thirty minutes. With remote work, turning my camera off allows me more time and space to recharge when corporate America is asking me, a human being, with deep, nuanced feelings, to operate as though I'm a robot. Remote work is especially clutch during my menstrual cycle. Once, early on in the pandemic, I had one of *those* cramps. You know, the kind that makes you feel like you're fighting the war on terror inside of your uterus, and because I was working from home I lay down. I didn't thug it out. I didn't go and hide in the bathroom. I didn't put on a stoic face while a blood clot the size of an iPod Shuffle passed through me. I turned my camera off, made sure I was on mute, and assumed the not helpful but very instinctual fetal position until the pain subsided. Had I been in the office, I would have had to perform my work duties and pretend like Thanos wasn't using Thor's hammer inside of me and pray to God I didn't soil my undergarments on top of that!

But what's most thrilling about working from home is not having to duck, dodge, or dive the microaggressions of whiteness. The safety I feel opening my laptop as I sit at my desk or kitchen table, whether barefoot or wearing socks or house slippers, cannot be quantified because I'm in my own space and it isn't being highjacked by the niceties Black folks must commence with when around mixed company. I want to be clear and state, yes, I do hate all white people. I cannot stand to be around y'all. (Kidding! Just wanted to see if you all were still with me.) I don't hate white folks, but I do loathe the dance I have to do around white people in corporate spaces because their safety, whether physical or emotional, is always centered and their wellness is always a top priority. It's seen in the way some managers will not take sides after blatant aggression or unprofessionalism has been displayed. This alleged neutrality isn't neutral at all. What's being communicated is that there's just enough room left for this uncouth behavior to continue and for the victim to remain victimized. When I'm working from home, I can put myself first, I can be safe, and the work still gets done. I can fire off emails, answer Slack messages, kill it in meetings, and not ever remove my bonnet or silk scarf. I once greased my entire scalp while simultaneously creating a pitch the client loved and bought. I can still effectively produce while twisting my locs or applying press-on nails without ever getting out of my robe. (A former colleague had his camera off and participated in a meeting while getting a shape up. The client bought the idea he pitched, and his hairline was crispy too.) And if I want to engage with my colleagues, I can do so when I feel like it by simply turning my camera on.

Working from home gives employees more freedom to divorce themselves from the unwritten rules that come with having to be in the office. Take, for example, "Sarah" from accounting (the one who never approves your expenses), who's leaving the company. Remote work means you don't *have* to attend the going-away party and, more importantly, you don't have to concern yourself with how it looks now that you didn't attend Sarah's going-away party. At work, you must look the part of being a team player even if other members on the team have never played fair. Working from home removes you from all of that. Another bonus of remote work is that it takes away the burden of ambition. As previously stated, a large part of being a working adult is looking happy to be there and not only performing your job function but being the "above and beyond" employee. Doing everything and anything necessary to get the job done and having a "can-do, scrappy" attitude is what recruiters look for and managers can't get enough of. But honestly, some of us just want to pay our rent, go to brunch, and maybe hit up Ghana once a year. When you're in the office, the energy needed to bring this performance to life can sometimes be more strenuous than doing the actual work. My late friend Jonathan once brilliantly said to me, "Don't let your ambition kill you. It's there to fuel you, not tire you out." Companies don't want to hear that you're there for the check so you can pay your bills and live. They want you to want to give your all. They want you to do what it takes. They believe the paycheck you've earned entitles them to enthusiasm. But that monetary compensation doesn't mean they're worthy of an emotional response from me.

Working remotely gave me the power to put all of that in a casket and bury it. Now, I can log in, keep my camera off, stay on mute, and simply do the job I was paid to do, and if on Monday I can give 100 percent, awesome. If on Tuesday, I'm sitting under a dryer with a plastic shower cap over my head doing a fifteen-minute deep condition, that's okay as well. The work is still getting done and my humanity or Blackness doesn't have to take a back seat.

I don't know what the future holds. As I write this, junior year of Covid is about to end. Mask mandates are a thing of the past and it feels like a lot of people think the worst of the pandemic is behind them. Companies that allowed remote work may demand that everyone come back to the office or at least offer employees a hybrid option. Maybe employers will learn from the past few years and take stock of the emotional needs of their staff, or maybe companies just need to make use of the commercial real estate. Either way, my hope is that employers consider their Black employees more and provide spaces where our Blackness can be full, bright, and nuanced. But, if this isn't an agenda item or can't be squeezed into the budget, then at least understand why some of us, myself included, will keep our cameras off when given the opportunity to do so.

7

Jagged Little Pill

My junior high school, M.S. 158, was directly across the street from my childhood home, which meant I could get an extra fifteen or twenty minutes of sleep in the morning and still make it to homeroom on time, but that also meant skipping school wasn't an option. At the end of the day, I'd walk through the front door and often hear the last of the *General Hospital* theme music or the beginning of the roaring studio audience clapping on *The Oprah Winfrey Show*. Some days my grandmother would look out the front kitchen window while washing dishes just to make sure I came straight home. On those days, Oprah was simply in the background and keeping her company. Other times, I'd walk in the house and she'd barely notice because her eyes were glued to the television screen.

Oprah, with her gorgeous deep-conditioned, well-trimmed black hair, interviewed everyone from Sidney Poitier to Nelson Mandela and even a couch-jumping Tom Cruise. But it was Iyanla Vanzant, lawyer, inspirational speaker, relationship coach, and author, who stood out. In the late '90s, Iyanla would stop by the show and give her counsel every other week or so. She'd be so captivating that even Oprah would take a seat and let her have the stage as she wowed the audience with her wisdom and warmth. Oprah may have given Iyanla a platform, but Ms. Vanzant commanded the attention from viewers.

Then, one week, Iyanla didn't show up, and for eleven years she wasn't on the show. As the story goes, Iyanla wanted her own daytime talk show, which makes sense. After a year or so of holding court in Oprah's playground, it's understandable that she'd want her own sandbox to play in. Oprah and the rest of the Harpo production team, however, thought she needed more time before she earned her place on center stage. So now at an impasse, the two parted ways behind closed doors. In 2010, Iyanla wrote and published her book *Peace from Broken Pieces* and returned to *The Oprah Winfrey Show* to promote it, but not before hashing out their past. On February 16, 2011, Iyanla, dressed in white with her ginger-colored short hair framing her face and megawatt smile, walked across the studio right into Oprah's arms and the two embraced. Gone from the stage was Oprah's couch and instead were two cream-colored chairs.

"I am now so sorry," Iyanla said, her voice full of humility and acceptance.

"I accept your apology," Oprah replied. "No apology necessary. You're already forgiven."

From the outside looking in, there seemed to be a sincere desire to give their disagreement a proper burial. A decade had passed and both women earnestly wanted to move forward, only bringing the lessons learned from their falling out with them. The conversation wasn't all warm and fuzzy, though. It weaved outside of the gentle and into the assertive with Iyanla making a claim about how their disagreement was handled, to which Oprah said something I will never forget.

"I will not accept that," Oprah asserted.[1]

Ms. Winfrey didn't raise her voice. She didn't roll her eyes. She didn't use an expletive. Clear, firm, and controlled, Oprah said: "I will not accept that." Oprah accepted Iyanla's apology, but she did not accept Iyanla's recollection of events, which to me was a first. I'd never heard anyone say that before, much less assert what they would and would not abide within a disagreement or confrontation. Up until that moment, I thought if someone was angry with you, you didn't have any rights. I didn't know you had a choice or any power in a situation in which you were thought to be wrong. I believed you had to accept whatever treatment the person dished out because they were mad at *you*. It's been years since that pivotal sit-down. Oprah and Iyanla have gone on to heal their personal relationship and have had a fruitful professional one. That moment between them has stayed with me because it was the first time I remember seeing two hurt people respectfully express their anger and disagree. Iyanla wasn't intimidated by Oprah's success, and Oprah wasn't about to let Iyanla just paint a narrative that best suited her story, but both women said their piece and did so with the intention of maintaining peace. The goal wasn't to hurt one another; it was to communicate and be understood. Hurt and anger are the Milli Vanilli of emotions, because hurt lip-syncs as anger, and anger oftentimes sets out to dish out the hurt it feels. People don't say "What you did really hurt me and my feelings." They instead yell, shove, sting, or punch. But this chapter and this book aren't about people and their relationship with hurt and anger. This is about me.

I'm both terrified of my anger and propelled by it. The two are tightly braided together and I work tirelessly to ensure not a hair is ever loose, mostly because I'm afraid of what coming undone would look like. Would my fury be glorious, like lava snaking its way down a volcano, or would it take on the clumpy texture and sour smell of vomit? Even before I could articulate it, I've always known that you cannot take back words once they've left your mouth, so while others felt emboldened to say what they wanted because they were angry, I've known that the fallout from expressing those ripe feelings isn't always an easy cleanup. Ironically, though, a significant part of my career has been fueled by anger. I wouldn't write about injustices or life's intentional imbalances if I weren't already irate about them, and in this regard, I've learned to hold hands and even dance with anger. When I use rage as ink to pen certain stories there's the safety net of the delete button, which waters my confidence. I can let my anger roar as loud as I want, and then delete a sentence or two that may have gone too far. When I write from a place of vexation, I know I don't have to deal with the full consequences because the delete button is there to protect me. Anger, as powerful an emotion as it is, is also a fleeting one that leaves lasting damage. But when I write, because I believe I can take it all back, there's a built-in policing that keeps me safe.

Unfortunately, there's no backspace in real life.

Just because you're a kind and respectful person doesn't mean you won't become the victim of someone's misplaced anger, and if you are intentionally rude, you can bet the fade will be FedEx'd to your home, overnight delivery and all. Yet somewhere along the way, I learned anger wasn't for me, not because anger didn't "come in my size," per se, but because as a girlchild and later a woman, it was "unbecoming" to express any emotion that wasn't neatly packaged behind a smile and good home training. I was supposed to absorb and tolerate all misunderstandings despite having a full understanding of the transgression that occurred. It was fine for others to incite and make me angry, yet to express a reactionary indignation often resulted in gaslighting: *Why you being so sensitive?* Or dismissiveness: *It's not even that serious, relax!*

It's a deliberate kind of cruelty when women aren't given the room to at least yell or shout about our frustrations. And if we do, it's judged not in relation to the offense and what led up to it; it's based on what someone outside of the circumstance deems "normal or appropriate." This clogging of a woman's anger or her right to express it without judgment can manifest itself in different ways. Maybe a woman shuts down and disengages, which is my brand of conflict resolution, or maybe she cries. The salty water that trickles down isn't always because she's tender or soft on the inside and her feelings are hurt. It could be because she'd like to punch you in your face, strangle you with your spine, or use your femur to knock you out. The tears are there because she knows she cannot inflict the same level of aggression—whether micro or macro—because then she'll be considered "emotional," and being emotional is a big no-no if you're a woman. There's also a safety component that may stop a lot of women from showing anger. If a man slaps my behind while walking down the block, it may not be prudent of me to punch him in the face, because while his act of sexual violence wholly merits a reaction, my counterattack could result in my demise. In order for a woman to even show anger, she has to, on some level, feel safe enough to express it, whether she's at the corner store or behind her desk in her corner office. One might not think anger and safety go hand in hand, but they do.

Going through these various social Hula-Hoops doesn't just happen with strangers or male colleagues. It can also occur with some of your closest homeboys. One day, I was on the phone with a friend who asked me how the chapters for my book were coming along. (Sidebar: Most writers hate when people ask, "How's the writing coming along?" *Why?* Because the writing is never coming along as smoothly or as quickly as we'd hoped. Writing is tough and it doesn't get any easier despite how many times you do it. So, if you know a writer, don't ask how the writing is coming along. Instead, change the subject to something more hopeful, like climate change or the fight to save koalas from extinction.) After working on my proposal for a year and then waiting the several agonizing months to learn an editor at a publishing house liked and bought it, I was thrilled that I had made it one step closer to becoming a published author. There's no guarantee that just because you're a writer you'll be able to make a living off it. The arts aren't as "stable" a career as say technology, medicine, or law, so to be given the greenlight that my book would one day be in bookstores was affirming and exciting. What I didn't know was that once an offer has been accepted, contract negotiations can take time, which can slow down receiving your advance. So, after working as hard as I did on my proposal, I was ready to be compensated.

"Actually, I haven't started working on it," I said.

"Why?" he asked.

"Well, because I haven't gotten my advance yet."

A beat.

"Wait, hold up. Do you *even* want to write this book?" he asked.

Confused, I responded, "Yes, of course. Why do you ask?"

"Because it sounds like you're only writing this book for money, which, I mean, is fine if you are . . ."

In my mind, whenever I hear of other women being insulted, my reactions are swift, clever, and full of as much venom as was unceremoniously bestowed. But when I'm the main character in a situation, seldom are my retorts as artistic as I hope them to be. It took me a minute, literally sixty seconds, to process what happened. In my friend's mind, not working on the chapters for my book diluted the gratitude I had for the position I was in. The "payment" was in the privilege to write; to squander any time I may have because I hadn't been compensated was an indicator this opportunity was nothing more than a financial play, a means of financing a trip to Essence Fest or SXSW, if you will. His comment stung, like alcohol in a fresh cut, because he's also a writer and his advance was cute. Maybe not enough to use as a down payment on a house cute, but it was definitely cuter than mine, so for him to say what he said pissed me off! Being a starving artist has been branded as the purest form of artistry. If you're willing to work simply for the love, then that will show through your art and make it better. But the idea of wanting to be compensated for the work you do somehow dilutes the creativity and the creative. You don't become a writer because you want to pay off your student loans, that's for damn sure, but it was insulting that my friend, who understands the publishing business, couldn't comprehend why I wanted my money! My little nickels and dimes weren't going to help me buy a Chanel purse or a necklace from Van Cleef & Arpels, but it would validate me as writer. Getting paid for my words means something and he of all people should know that. Was I supposed to write this book from the kindness of my heart? Was I supposed be so fulfilled by being given a seat at the author table that payment should've been furthest from my mind? According to my friend, yes!

"How dare you?" I said over the phone, my blood at a rapid boil.

"What?" he responded.

"How dare you question the integrity I have for my book simply because I want my advance."

"It just sounds like . . ."

"I don't care what you think it sounds like, you twat! You have no right."

"Whoa!" he said. "All I'm saying, Shenequa—"

"Yo, are you serious, right now? I'm off this, for real," I yelled before hanging up.

He really had no idea how insulting his words were and, dare I say it, he may have thought he was being helpful. I called Ashleigh afterward to explain everything and asked if my reaction had been over the top. While I knew what I felt, I wasn't necessarily convinced that me cussin' him out was the right course of action.

"Shenequa, why do you need me to cosign your feelings? If you tight, then you tight, and that's just what it's gon' be! You're allowed to be angry," she said.

If you're taking a math test, you know that two plus two equals four. That math is right, but if someone questions your integrity and your motives, is it "correct" to call said person a twat? (I'm unsure where on the Black girl math spectrum twat-name-calling lands.) Should I have politely excused myself from the conversation to cool down? Maybe I should've slapped the mess out of him with a dirty pair of black Air Force Ones had this happened in person? As these questions ran through my mind, I needed a friend to corroborate my feelings and tell me: "Yes, Shenequa! He was out of pocket."

About a week later he reached back out. I didn't bother going into details with him. I wasn't still upset, but I was fatigued. It's disappointing to think that even though he's the one who caused the offense, I still had to explain why his words were hurtful and disrespectful. It was double the emotional work and I had no interest.

"You cool?" he asked. "I didn't really understand why you were so upset."

"Yeah, I'm cool," I responded.

. . .

Research shows there are four stages of anger: annoyance, frustration, hostility, and rage.[2]

Annoyance can be losing your new concealer, while *frustration* is the viral video of Hazel London and her homegirl standing in the parking lot outside of Bella Noche. *Hostility* happens when someone has repeatedly been disrespected or disregarded, hence why so many New Yorkers would fight the MTA if they could, and *rage* is the final stage. If annoyance, frustration, and hostility decided to form Destiny's Child, rage would still be Beyoncé's Coachella performance. The trio helps create or at least funnel into rage and gives it a platform to let loose. If not properly managed, rage can include intense verbal confrontations and physical altercations. Rage may also be learning the author of this book lied and that koalas aren't facing extinction after all.

Annoyance is an emotion I feel often because I'm super type A, which means lots of spreadsheets and "just following up on my previous email." I'm also deeply attached to perfectionism. When you've been made to feel wrong, the natural defense is to ensure you're always right. In my mind, if I do everything perfectly, then nothing can or should go awry. (My therapist and I are working on this.) So, whenever something does go left, as is the case with Monday mornings, missed deadlines, or life in general, I get annoyed, because things aren't as perfect as I prepared or wanted them to be. There's a deep satisfaction, a security, and a confidence boost that comes with having executed something without a hiccup. Yet, when things aren't flawless or they're incorrect, that means something needs to be fixed or adjusted. And after exerting all that effort to achieve perfection, I have little energy left to fix anything. Perfectionism, while unachievable, is also exhausting and leaves little room to rebound, which is also why it's such a lost cause. I also get annoyed when people substitute the "N" for an "M" in Valentine's Day, or when my mom asks me what's the weather like despite both of us having an iPhone and neither of us having stepped outdoors.

Annoyance is a frequent emotion in my life, but it also has a short life span. Frustration, however, comes knocking whenever someone else's foolishness now becomes my problem. I'm most frustrated either on my way to work (this was pre-COVID) or while at work. So, if I wake up on time, get dressed, my locs are kind of cooperating and my makeup looks cute, I get frustrated if the train has come to a standstill because of a sick passenger. I'm aware that this is horrible, but the first thought that comes to my mind is, *Why did this person decide to get sick on my train?* Couldn't the person have transferred and let their pathogens link up with its other pathogen homies someplace else, like on the G train, perhaps? The G train goes to Hogwarts. Everyone knows this.

In the rare cases when the MTA isn't trying to ruin my life and the lives of fellow New Yorkers, frustration can take the form of someone else dropping the ball, but now I'm responsible for catching it before it shatters on the ground. That often looks like having to complete a project in half the time it usually takes because it was promised to a client. It doesn't matter how much of an inconvenience this task is or how many priorities must be shifted in order to deliver. Someone else made the call and now I have to deal with it. I also get frustrated when my coffee isn't good, whether because I purchased a bad cup at Starbucks or the pot I brewed wasn't vibes. If I didn't take coffee seriously this could end up in the annoyance column, but since coffee is life, bad coffee is beyond frustrating. Good coffee isn't just coffee; it's the liquid version of your boss calling to give you Monday off. That ease, that delight, that sudden jolt of energy because goodness has entered your bloodstream, coffee is all those things and more, but you already know this because you read chapter 5. Frustration also pops up when people choose not to use manners. I grew up in a West Indian household, and "good morning," "good evening," and "good night," along with "yes, please," "no thank you," "excuse me," or "beg pardon?" could mean the difference between you living to see another day or not, so for people to just exist without having any proper home training frustrates me to no end.

I become hostile when I learn about blatant forms of corruption or injustice that are being committed and tolerated.

So, when Roe v Wade was overturned you were . . .

Beyond words.

The shock, anger, and literal terror took away my ability to process what happened. I've been assaulted twice, and it was because of the grace of God those assaults didn't result in a pregnancy. What was the Supreme Group Chat doing to help prevent or lower sex crimes? Nothing, but denying women the right to do what they wanted or in some cases medically needed to do with their bodies was now law.

Rage isn't a feeling I dance with often, but when I do it's usually in the past tense. I'm rageful when I think of the times I was taken advantage of or lacked the courage to speak up for myself. Like sophomore year of high school when I tried confronting the twins Michelle and Melissa. I wouldn't call them popular, but they knew more people than I did, which meant they had more social currency. I can't remember what the beef was about, but I foolishly had assumed a calm dialogue full of healing between three high school–aged teens could be had. Instead, I was ambushed by their twin power and made a fool of while in Cardozo High School's main corridor, which we nicknamed 42nd Street because of how crowded it became when students changed classes. I was overpowered and woefully unprepared for how sharp and fast their mean-girlness exploded. I stuttered and tripped over the few words I was able to get out, while they threw their acid-filled language at my self-esteem. And when they were done ripping me apart, they turned to Kimberly, Camile, and the rest of the crowd watching and boldly said "Who's next?" I should've known then that Kim and Cam weren't my real friends. They did nothing to help or defend me in that moment. They stood there useless and silent like the letter *l* in the word "salmon." Reflecting on this moment also brings about such disappointment. Had I possessed even a modicum of insight or wisdom I would've severed ties with both of them right then.

If I could go back in time and defend high school me, I'd tell the twins that their breath stinks and the mustache above their lips is getting out of hand. I would also tell twentysomething Shenequa, *You have just as much power as those other bitches, if not more.* Swallowing jagged little pills, bearing the burden of them rubbing together and scratching against your larynx and esophagus just to keep quiet, has done you no favors. I might mentally revisit an incident or retell a story, and it's only in the furrowing of someone's eyebrows, the slight tilt of their head, or the confused expression on their face that lets me know what I assumed was normal behavior wasn't normal at all. Thinking back on the times when someone played me, and I let it slide because I wasn't swift enough to catch the disrespect or because I wanted to keep the peace, causes me to now perform double duty. I have to contend with the past version of myself for accepting the behavior in the first place, while managing the ripe anger and cringing embarrassment that comes from how easily I wilted and question why I didn't fight back. Why didn't I speak up? Why was I so hellbent on being the bigger person? What's the point in keeping the peace if my hurt feelings are part of the "peace treaty"? The safe answer is: Why waste your time and energy? I've seen people retaliate and express their anger, and even in moments when they were right, oftentimes they're the ones who end up with high blood pressure! But the truth is, I've never felt like I had a right to fight back against someone's anger because if the person is upset with me then, *clearly*, I did something wrong, and because I'm wrong, I deserve their harsh treatment.

I recently had a falling out with a close friend who leveled a huge and offensive charge against me. When she made this accusation, she didn't calmly explain her stance. Instead, she put on a showstopping display of ugliness, calling me every name except the one my mother gave me. During her barrage of insults—*"Bitch, you really think I give a fuck!"*—I was not only taken aback, but I thought I deserved this tongue-lashing, because obviously I had done something *wrong* to merit it. It was only weeks later after having mentally cycled through the incident for the hundredth time that I realized not only was she incorrect, but I had more than enough justification to fight back. The moment between us was gone, and she'd already blocked my number, so I spoke my piece in the best way I could, via an email.

> *You so easily used disrespect as a weapon*
> *against me, which can only lead me to believe*
> *you suddenly lost respect for me or have always*
> *been secretly harboring resentment toward me.*
>
> *I have not always been a good friend to other people.*
> *I can own this, but to you, I tried my best and for you*
> *to tear me apart was a gut punch I couldn't prepare*
> *for because it wasn't something I expected.*[3]

Her response only deepened the knife in my heart.

LOL, Shenequa . . .

What did you hope to accomplish here?
Because I'm truly at a loss.

Did you want to try and make me feel bad about
being angry and ugly toward you? Cause I don't.[4]

And then it hit me: Me feeling as if I was wrong prevented me from speaking up in the moment, while she thinking she was right emboldened her to not only express her anger but to be mean about it. "Being right" meant that her rage was justified and so was the disrespect. My sore feelings aside, her vicious speech taught me who I don't want to be and how I don't want to conduct myself. Anger has its place, for sure. In certain situations and moments, it's a reasonable response. How one expresses that anger is a different story. I never want to be like my one-time friend: someone who feels entitled in hurting someone or their feelings simply because they're upset, and they *believe* they're right. It's easy to fly off the handle, cuss someone out, raise your blood pressure, and have the last word. (My doctor told me my blood pressure was 123 over 76 and I am so proud of me! This is such a flex.) But it takes a mature person to express anger and hurt in a way that can be understood, and to do that requires wanting to move past the situation and not wanting to inflict harm.

The way my one-time friend chose to detail her feelings is something that's widely perceived as effective and, most importantly, powerful. Demonstrating anger in a disrespectful way is intended to make the other person feel and look small, which is what she did when she cussed me out and then again when she noted she didn't care about cussing me out or hurting my feelings.

"Did you want to try and make me feel bad about being angry and ugly toward you? Cause I don't."

She didn't want to be understood; she wanted to be bigger than me. She didn't want us to come to an agreement, even if that agreement was to go our separate ways. She wanted to inflict pain, which is painful, but it showed me how different we are. This might sound arrogant, but I don't regularly feel small, nor do I on a daily basis feel like I have to show someone how big I am. Iyanla and Oprah endured enough hurt during their eleven-year sabbatical from one another. When they finally reconnected, they wanted to close the door on that chapter in the healthiest way possible. That, unfortunately, wasn't my experience. My friend didn't just close the door in my face; she intentionally wanted to jam my finger.

I'm still not entirely sure where I land when it comes to anger and how I will express mine when the time comes. It's hard to maintain your cool when someone's in your face, calling you this and that, but I also don't want to be the person in someone else's face calling them this or that. I don't feel the need to show people with rage, theatrics, cuss words, and whatever else folks who allege "I'm not the one" do. That doesn't look or make me feel like I'm ten feet tall. Maybe this realization proves that I, inherently, am the bigger person. Defining what power means to me and how I will wield it may take me a bit longer. This weird middle ground I've found myself in doesn't sound conclusive, and may even merit a shoulder shrug, but it does feel like progress, because I'm no longer cowering, and you know what, I'm not mad at it.

8

Daddy's Girl

Saturday morning cartoons were one of the best parts about growing up for most '80s babies and '90s kids. Along with being the official start of the weekend, it set the tone for whatever fun would unfold throughout the day. When it was raining out, these cartoons provided a bit of sunshine and joy even though we were stuck indoors. For parents who couldn't function before ten or eleven in the morning, these thirty-minute animated TV shows acted as a free babysitter, keeping children safe, quiet, and occupied while they received a few extra winks of sleep. Like most kids, I poured a big bowl of sugary cereal. I was partial to Apple Jacks or Corn Pops, and I sat quietly in front of the television thoroughly entertained by the fun and foolishness on display. Shows like *Tiny Toon Adventures*, *Rugrats*, *Darkwing Duck*, *X-Men*, and *Pinky and the Brain* were some of the top-tier animations I watched growing up. Yet, for me, one cartoon stood out among the pack and that was *Gargoyles*.

The animated series lasted three seasons, but it had everything that made for great television. There was a fire-ass origin story dating back to Scotland 994 AD, a bit of mysticism, loss, betrayal, not so thinly veiled prejudice, a clever and honest-hearted NYPD detective (who was half-Black, by the way), and some rich white man with an impressive ponytail-goatee combo who had enough money to buy a distressed castle in Scotland and transport it to a Manhattan skyscraper. While *Gargoyles* wasn't originally a part of the prestigious Saturday morning cartoon lineup, it belongs within the conversation of great cartoons of the '90s. I watched *Gargoyles* every time it came on and loved how chubby Broadway was and thought Bronx was such a cute name for the gargoyle dog. I also remember watching *Gargoyles* when Mommy told me my father was coming to pick me up after school, but he never showed.

It was a Friday afternoon when I flung off my bookbag after coming home from school. I might've been eight or nine at the time, but I remember tiptoeing to reach the top of the refrigerator to get a box of cereal, and then a bowl from a nearby cabinet. Friday afternoons meant I didn't have to rush and start my homework; I could sit at my kitchen table, which had a small television, and enjoy whatever adventure Hudson, Goliath, and the rest of the pack got themselves into. The cherry on top was I'd be with my father in a few hours. Soon, the Defenders of the Night, as the gargoyles were known as, turned to stone, signaling the end of the show. Another cartoon came on after, so I watched it, still excited about spending time with my father, but then that cartoon ended, and then another and then another and pretty soon I was watching the "TGIF" lineup.

"Hey, Mommy," I said when she came home from work later that evening. "Did my father call?"

"No, Chin Chin," she said somberly. "He didn't. Maybe he got caught up with something. He'll probably come tomorrow."

I didn't have any reason to not believe Mommy, and as a kid with no working definition of disappointment, I assumed my dad must've gotten busy with something else, and he would for sure show up the next day. Saturday morning arrived and the milk from my new bowl of Apple Jacks turned a faint pink. I still hadn't lost hope. My heart jumped every time the phone rang because I wanted it to be him telling me he was on his way. Instead, it was a call for my cousins Tisha or Andre or someone else in the house.

"Hey, Mommy, did my father call you at work?" I asked when she returned home that afternoon.

"No, Chin," she said.

"Oh. Okay," I responded.

"You want to go to McDonald's and jump in the ball pit?"

"Yeah!" I said excitedly. "And by the time we come back, he'll be here."

Mommy drove to the McDonald's on Northern Boulevard, where she most likely ordered the Number 2 that came with two cheeseburgers, fries, a drink and, for another dollar, two apple pies. This one meal was enough to split between the both of us. While she carried the tray of food to an empty table, I ran upstairs to the Play Place, kicked off my shoes, and jumped into the ball pit, surrounded by an ocean of red, yellow, blue, and green plastic balls. I came up for air and swam in the sea of toys and fun, totally believing that after lunch with Mommy, I'd spend time with my father.

As a little girl, I had this unrelenting optimism in my father that now as an adult I find admirable. It was fueled by a deep longing to be wanted by him. I wanted my father to hug me, kiss me, and tell me about his day and ask about mine. I wanted us to have our own thing, maybe it was a handshake or an inside joke or on Thursdays we'd get ice cream or something. I didn't need him to buy me a Barbie dollhouse or a new pair of rollerblades; I just wanted *him*, and because I wanted my father,

I held onto optimism. Letting go of that sparkly hope would've hurt more than accepting him not showing up.

And so it went for most of my childhood and into my teens. He'd say he was coming to hang out, and it was a crapshoot if he actually showed. But what he lacked in emotional offerings he "made up for" financially. He bought me my first computer, which I used to play a nauseating amount of solitaire on, and when Britney Spears's debut album was released, I popped that CD in and rocked out. (Black girls love Britney Spears, and real ones know her perfume Curious was bomb!) I wrote some of my early poems and stories on that computer. I thought my writing was deep, pure, and edgy, when it was mostly nonsensical and full of typos. The gifts were initially a source of comfort because they were a tangible representation of what I wanted, which was his attention, and so not having him, his time, or his love made these gifts feel like I was getting *something* from him. So yes, initially these items did fill an emotional hole. But soon, my father's materialistic responses to the emotions he couldn't, wouldn't, or didn't know how to offer became too apparent to ignore. Even to this day, men who offer gifts don't sit well with me. When it came to my dad, I could no longer appreciate or care about these trinkets. It felt like my father believed all he had to do was throw money or gifts at his child and that meant he was a good parent. My father had no problem disappointing me because, in his mind, aren't gifts a great consolation prize for a kid? Sometimes he'd give Mommy money for new school clothes and supplies, but the warmth, attention, and true desire to invest in me weren't there.

When I was about eleven, Mommy told me to get dressed because my father was taking me to breakfast. My optimism hadn't totally dwindled by that point and when he actually arrived, his presence fortified why I should still believe in him. My father is reserved but has a commanding presence, something I've been told I also possess. He's tall, about six-foot-two inches with a booming voice and hearty laugh. Yet when he speaks, he puts you at ease. Seated inside of his white Mercedes Benz, I remember feeling like I had stepped into a spaceship. It was my first time in his car and a luxury one at that. The fairy-tale of the moment made real by the soft peanut butter–colored seats was briefly disrupted by the strewn-about newspaper in the back. It didn't matter though because my father still had a Benz. Mommy didn't have a fancy car and that not-so-subtle difference watered a baseless belief that formed inside of me: Life with my father had certain perks that life with Mommy on Oceania Street couldn't offer. My father lived an opulent life with fancy cars. For Mommy and me, we took the Q31 to Jamaica Avenue when we needed to shop, and going to Mc-Donald's was considered a treat.

When we got to the diner, I couldn't contain my excitement. Something about having one-on-one time with my father felt more thrilling than any roller-coaster ride. Growing up, I wasn't the kid who had the fly clothes or who earned all the awards in school. I was kind of in the middle. I was good at some things and not so great at others. Who I was and what I was experiencing were all things I wanted to talk to my father about. Maybe because it was such a rarity to have him around or because being with him made *me* feel important, whatever the reason, the joy was bursting out of me. I sat on my hands kicking my legs under the table barely missing my father's knees as he sat across from me. He was here. It was *really* happening.

"Good morning, y'all," our waitress said, pulling her note-pad out of an apron pocket. "What can I start you two off with?"

"Can I have an orange juice, please?" I said, my legs going wild under the table. "But not the kind that has those stringy thingies in it."

"Pulp, sweetie?" the waitress responded.

"Yeah, that," I said.

"A coffee for me," my father ordered.

"Cream and sugar alright, sir?" the waitress asked.

"Yeah, that's fine."

"Okay, I'll be right back with your drinks."

"No need. We already know what we want."

After we placed our orders, the waitress walked away still jotting down notes on her notepad. And then my father leaned to the side to retrieve his neatly folded newspaper, the one strewn about in his car, from his back pocket and began reading the sports section.

"Why didn't you get waff—" I began to ask.

"Hold on, Chin," he said with his head stuck in the paper.

In that moment, I could hear the clanging of pots and pans from the kitchen, cooks shouting to staff their orders were ready, chatter from parents at neighboring tables trying to simmer down their rambunctious kids, but at our booth, all I heard was the soft crinkle of the newspaper. My father's eyes were opened wide as he read about whatever game happened the night before. He didn't just skim the headline or briefly glance at a page or two. My father *read* the newspaper, which would be normal, almost admirable, if it hadn't come at the expense of spending time with his daughter. Once the silence fully set in at the booth, my legs stopped swinging under the table.

"Here you go," the waitress said bringing our drinks and dropping a duet of straws in between my orange juice, water, and his cup of coffee. "Your food should be right up. We're scrambling the eggs now."

I tried getting my father's attention, telling him about school, my friends and how bad I was at math, but he never acknowledged me or the conversation I was trying to have. He kept his head stuck in the paper and all but dismissed me. A minute or so later, our food arrived and whatever hope I had for any real time spent was out the door. There wasn't even a "How's your pancakes?" inquiry. It was him, his food, and his paper. This moment stuck with me because despite not having the language or the emotional intelligence at the time, I knew my father believed he did enough. He said he was taking me to breakfast and that's what he did. This time, he kept his word. He picked me up, kept me safe, fed me, and dropped me off back home. My father had filled his parental quota for the day. I shouldn't have had any complaints; the quality time I was hoping for was just that, a hope. But it felt as though he considered himself a "good dad" that day.

All throughout my teens and into young adulthood, my father popped in and out of my life, never taking the initiative to check in on or call, only responding to requests from Mommy for financial assistance. Our conversations thinned over time as my hope and optimism turned into resentment. I knew I was supposed to be cared for, but my father's approach to parenting echoed that of an on-call retail worker who may or may not be called in for their shift. Mommy never spoke ill of my father. In fact, she'd try to act as a mediator of sorts, telling me how alike we were. She'd say I got my height, my chubby cheeks, and my loner attitude all from him. The running joke on Oceania Street was that all I had to do was grow a beard and I'd be his twin. Mommy had the emotional burden of honoring my father by being respectful of him. Her grand prize for being the parent who stayed was trying to ease the blow from the parent who left.

I was in my early twenties by the time I graduated from Hampton University. At this stage in our "relationship" I viewed my father with the same familiarity as a neighbor. *"Good morning. How you doin'? Everything good? Alright. Take care."* There were bushels of small talk whenever he did call, but those instances were few and far between—and from my perspective, it was all performative. I got my first editorial job maybe two months after graduation and moved to Chicago. After getting acquainted with the ferocious winter and trying my best to make a name for myself as a young journalist, I didn't feel beholden to give my father anything other than the cordial pleasantries you give to someone you don't really know but you do recognize. He and I maintained such a healthy distance for such a long time, I would only think of him if someone brought up the subject of fathers. As a child, my father was an emotional priority who remained in the front of my mind. As a young twentysomething adult, my father was in the attic of my head and heart. An entire decade passed with no significant positive input from my father. He didn't teach me how to change a tire in the event my car broke down on the side of the road, nor did he show me how to peep game or spot the red flags while dating. Whatever knowledge or life experience he may have had, he didn't share with me, so I simply had to make do.

While working at my first journalism gig, a small paper owned by the *Chicago Sun-Times*, I quickly learned that municipal board meetings where decisions about the placement of a new stop sign or stop light were made weren't really my speed. (Pun low-key intended.) After three years of living the inverted-pyramid life, I quit and moved back to Queens. I worked retail by day to keep a few dollars in my pocket and applied to every editorial job I could find at night. Life was rough, and every day I wondered if I was wasting time pursuing a career as an entertainment writer, but eventually I started making progress. What was once radio silence to my applications soon turned into: "Hi, Ms. Golding. We reviewed your resume and clips, and while we think you're a strong candidate, we've decided to go in another direction. Best of luck to you." Yes, it was rejection, but at least I was getting a response, which at the time was an indicator I was getting close.

Eventually, I applied to the right job and received an email inquiring into when I would be free for a fifteen-minute first-round phone interview. I practically jumped out of my skin! After months of trying to claw my way into the industry, I now had a chance to actually *be* a writer. But never forget, the devil is always busy. It was 2011 and at the time I was team Android. For whatever reason, my charging port was on the fritz. Sometimes I'd plug it in, and my battery would be fully charged and then after a ten-minute call, it would plummet to 7 percent. I called my cell phone provider, gave them the spiel, and with insurance, they'd be able to overnight a new phone to me. I would just need to pony up one hundred dollars. I was three years removed from college and was making pennies working at Zara. I could barely afford a weekly MetroCard to get to work, much less the hundred dollars needed for a cheaper phone or a replacement. The only person who could help was Mommy. So, after charging my phone again, I gave her a ring.

"Mommy, ohmygod! Ohmygod! I have a job interview this week," I rambled.

"That's great, Chin!" she said. "Did you wash the dishes like I told you to?"

"Ma, forget about the dishes. Did you hear what I said? I have a job interview!"

"Chin, hold on, a customer's coming in," she said before switching to her professional voice, "Hi, how are you? Do you have a fitting today? What's the last name? Goldstein? What? Say that again? Oh, Goldman. Okay. Got it."

She returned to me. "Chin? Alright, we're in the biz! You've got an interview," she said.

"The only thing is my phone won't hold a charge. Luckily, I have insurance. All I need is one hund—"

"Aht! Aht!" Mommy said. "You need what now?"

"I just need one hundred dollars, and they'll be able to send me a new phone."

"Chin, I love you, but I don't have an extra hundred dollars to give you to buy a new phone."

"But Mommy," I said sheepishly. "This is my big chance. I'm calling from my cell now and I'm barely at 10 percent. The interview is this week! C'mon, Mommy."

"Chin," now with more steel than sugar in her voice, "I do not have any extra money. I just paid the rent, and the car note is due Friday. If you need a new phone, call your father. Let him give you the money."

Mommy hung up the phone and my cell died immediately afterward. I threw it on the couch and quickly followed suit by throwing myself on it as well. Despite my feelings, I got it. Mommy was tired of footing the financial and emotional bills that came with a then struggling writer. On my days off from Zara, she'd leave for work in the morning and see me sitting on the couch, only to come back home that evening and see me in the same exact spot. The couch in our two-bedroom apartment became my bedroom and office because my grandmother, now in her late seventies, occupied my old high school room. On top of providing for me, she was also the primary caregiver when it came to granny and her advancing dementia.

Some days Grandma was chill and other days we would watch her like she was a toddler. Mommy never asked me for a dime while I was trying to establish myself and my career. So, with everything she was already giving me, along with the responsibility of Grandma, I understood why asking her to invite Ben Franklin to the party was too much. If it's my dream to become a writer, then it's my responsibility to make it happen. If that meant getting a new phone, I'd better figure out how to do it on my own. Using the house phone definitely wasn't an option. Some days it sounded like the person calling was on the highest volume ever, and other days it sounded like the person on the other end of the line was dialing in from Jupiter.

I emailed my prospective employer and set up a call for the following week, which meant I had seven days to convince Mommy to give me the money she didn't have. I begged and pleaded and every time I tried to broach the subject, she'd respond: "Call your father." I hated the idea of needing him, but I knew I'd be a fool for not asking. I may be dumb, but I'm damn sure not stupid, and I knew if I wanted that gig, I had to call my father. So, one day, inside of our local Fairway grocery market, standing in front of the hot bar, I borrowed Mommy's cell and dialed his number. My father's syrupy baritone filled my ear. We made awkward small talk befitting of a father and daughter with no relationship. I explained my predicament, piqued with excitement that an employer was giving me an opportunity to become a *real* writer.

"The only thing is my phone can't hold a charge. I've had it for less than a year. I called up insurance and they said if I send them one hundred dollars, I can get a new phone," I said.

A beat.

"May I please have a hundred dollars?" I asked with more shame in my voice than I knew how to hide.

"Oh, Chin," he said with a weighted sigh. "I wish I could, I really do, but I don't have it right now."

"It's okay," I said halfheartedly. "I understand."

"Next time," he said.

"Mmmhmm," I replied.

I don't remember how we ended the conversation. I may have been with Mommy while she paid for the groceries or even when we put them in the back of her car. What I do remember was instantly feeling a switch being turned off. Prior to that moment, despite my resentment and our distance, there was a teeny-tiny part of that little girl left inside of me who hoped one day my father would get it and show up. He would wake up, understand the error of his ways, and try his best to make up for lost time. The awkwardness in our relationship would melt away as we got to know one another and then everything would be good. But that was never going to happen because for nearly twenty years my father had a chance to try, and he didn't. So, after he proved he couldn't emotionally step up to the plate and then him not financially helping either, something inside of me clicked. My father will never be the man I need or want him to be, and when I finally sat with this realization, I didn't cry. I didn't mope. I just accepted the truth. My phone remained on the fritz up until the interview and thankfully stayed charged long enough for me to get the job. With my first check, I bought a weekly MetroCard and got the phone from insurance myself.

. . .

About five years ago, my homegirl Grace asked if she could spend the night at my then Brooklyn apartment. She lived uptown at the time and had an early flight the next morning. Catching an Uber or Lyft from my place to the airport would've been a lot easier, faster, and cheaper. Once she arrived, she threw her heather-gray duffel bag on the floor, kicked off her shoes, and made a beeline for my refrigerator to chill a six-pack of Red Stripe she had brought as a token of her appreciation.

We didn't have much to catch up on because we spoke almost daily, but it was still good to have her nearby.

"You want a beer?" she asked about an hour later. "I think they should be cold now."

"Why not?" I said.

Grace returned to the couch with two beers and used her key-chain bottle opener to remove the caps from both.

"Cheers!" she said.

"Cheers!"

"Hey, have you ever been to Jamaica? Like, seen where your mom and dad grew up?" she asked.

"Oh yeah, I was four the first time I went. I was with my aunt, and I saw where my mom was raised and everything. You think East New York is crazy; Kingston is wild!"

"What about your dad?" she said before taking another swig.

"Oh," I said, then paused. "I don't know where he grew up."

"You don't talk about him much. What's he like?"

"You're right," I said, placing the beer on a coaster. "I don't talk about my dad often, but there's really nothing to discuss. He wasn't around often when I was a kid. In and out every now and then. He wasn't a permanent fixture in my life, but you're Caribbean too. You know how West Indian men are. They don't take care of their kids," I said, picking up my beer.

A beat.

"Nah, don't put that on all West Indian fathers," Grace said. "Your dad *chose* not to be in your life. West Indian men can be trash, you already know I know, but some of them are good dads."

As I sat on my burgundy couch, suddenly the only noise in my apartment was the laughter from my next-door neighbors enjoying the summer evening on their porch, creeping in through my cracked living room window. Grace's comment was devoid of malice, hurt, and even pitch. She said it matter-of-factly, kind of like she was giving directions.

Take a right at the Dunkin' Donuts. Drive up two blocks. Take a left and then another quick right at the light, and your dad chose not to be in your life.

In that moment, Grace helped me realize the magnitude of my father's rejection. At some point my father wanted a white Mercedes Benz and he worked to get it. I don't know how hard or how long he had to work for it, but, eventually, he became the owner of that luxury vehicle. My father didn't want to build a relationship with me, so the scraps he gave were all the emotional effort he thought I was worth, and that was a smack to the face. It was a smack not to my face as an adult but to the hopeful little girl who swung her legs wildly under the table. Thankfully, Grace received a text from a guy she was seeing, which helped pivot the conversation. She smiled the kind of smile you only have in the beginning of a relationship when everything is new, exciting, and possible. Eventually, she fell asleep on the pull-out couch, and I got some shut-eye in my room. The next morning, I made us both coffee and we chatted a bit before her Lyft arrived. After Grace left, I didn't think any more about her observation regarding my father because I had accepted my father's abandonment of me a long time ago.

I don't have anything left to give him. I don't have anger, hope, joy, curiosity, or even love. My indifference is a result of his deliberate lack. My father decided not to give much emotional effort and I, in turn, am doing the same. This might read hypocritically or as though I'm lacking in self-awareness.

It's not lost on me that I've devoted a chapter to him, but I've had thirty-plus years to make do with his nothingness. There wasn't anything I could do to make my father want to be in my life. Not good grades, not first place in spelling bees, nothing, and I've made peace with that. Through tears and years of questioning my own self-worth, I've come to accept him and the scraps he fed his daughter.

The worst part is the robust numbness I feel as I write these words. Emptiness would be too grand a word because it would mean that at one point I was full. I was never poured into by my father, so to give up on him feels natural and, to a certain degree, long overdue. I'm aware that our parents are people and people are inherently imperfect, but I don't even know my father's good qualities to buffer against his imperfections. There's a porcupine-ness about me that I think I've adopted from my father not being there. If I don't let people get too close, when they leave, it won't hurt so much. As forthcoming as I am I still hold and love even the dearest people in my life at a distance. On the flip side of things, I don't know what kind of woman I'd be if my father *were* in my life. Would I be as independent? Would I make better dating choices? Would I have figured out things earlier in life? I don't know. It's unfortunate, sad, and disappointing, but wanting him to be someone he isn't is a waste of time.

If I could talk to little Chin Chin, I wouldn't sugarcoat anything. I'd put my arm around her shoulder and hug her tight. I'd tell her that he isn't going to change. He won't get better and his love for you won't be shown in a way that you can latch on to, if it exists at all. I would tell her it will hurt for as long as you allow it to hurt you, which tasks you with an unfair responsibility at such a young age but will be good practice later on in life. But I'd then advise her to look around at those who are in her life. Everyone who ever called Oceania Street home are the ones who love you, care for you, and deserve your unwavering loyalty. Look to them for your definition of care and savor how love doesn't leave you longing for more, like your father. Instead, notice how love shows up every day, willing and eager to participate in your life, especially now as a child. Whether it be the first day of kindergarten at P.S. 31 or your graduation from Hampton University. Love is Andre picking you up from preschool or Tisha taking you to Harlem to get your hair braided because Alicia Keys just came out and you want braids just like her. It's Auntie Lavern (pronounced LUH-veRn) never holding it over your head that you threw up in her brand-new car on the ride home from the hospital as a newborn or the many dinners Grandma cooked while Mommy was at work. Let this example be the blueprint you attach yourself to when defining and searching for love. So, when this episode of *Gargoyles* is over, Chin Chin, don't stay in the house and wait for him. Go outside, play and laugh. Don't be afraid to practice jumping in the rope while playing Double Dutch. You already know how to turn. Just time it, wait for the rope to go up and then jump in.

Go experience as much joy as you can, Chin Chin.

9

Raincheck

There's an old picture of me and my two cousins, Tisha, and Andre, sitting at the table for Christmas dinner. I was wearing one of my many Uncle Phil–like sweaters Mommy bought me, and my hair was in three or four big plaits. Tisha had on a denim button-down, jeans, and gold hoop earrings. Her soft black hair in a loose bun and her smooth brown skin aglow from an apparent application of Vaseline. Andre wore a freshly ironed gray collared shirt under a black, gray, and red argyle sweater. With his mischievous grin, he tipped his snapback as he sat at the head of the table, his back against the wood paneling that separated the foyer from the kitchen. Tisha and Andre, ten and twelve years old respectively, were your average kids happy about Christmas Day and even happier about the food that would soon be in their bellies.

I, however, was over it.

In the picture, I'm slouched in the red velvet seat looking up, and in my eyes it's clear I'm done. The white rice and brown stew chicken on the table weren't enough to spruce me up or even get me to smile. Baby Chin Chin was ready to go! Thirty years later, Tisha sent me a screengrab of the photo after Andre sent it to her. I don't know where Andre found it,

but seeing it brought back so many memories of life on Oceania Street. I could smell the sautéed onions in the thick gravy
used to smother the chicken, and I could feel the steam that
filled the kitchen from the pot full of cooked white rice. I also
couldn't help but laugh. Some kids have an undeniable bounce
and bubble to them, especially on Christmas Day. I was not
that child.

When I showed Mommy the now bent and partly discol-
ored photograph, she tried to offer an alternative account, alleging that my visible detachment from the family fun could've
been due to being woken up from a nap or about due for one.
Mommy was generous and even kind with her revisionist account of Christmas Day in 1988, but anyone who knows me
knows that being alone is my safety net, canceled plans are my
drug of choice, and skipping out early is my modus operandi.
I'm ready to go before I've even left the house.

Growing up, I wasn't allowed to go outside often and if I
did go out and play, I didn't have the luxury of staying out long.
Mommy was protective about who I hung out with and where
I went, even if it was just up the block and around the corner at
Marie Curie Playground. I usually had to be back home within
an hour, and that was her being generous. How I was able to
make friends within sixty-minute increments is beyond me, but
I did it. A tight leash is what she kept me on and if there's one
feeling I remember most about my childhood, it was salivating
for the day when I turned eighteen so I could do whatever I
wanted. Mommy was strict so it was either come home when
she said or remain trapped in the house like Rapunzel (except
with box braids).

Growing up, I *hated* Mommy's rules because they felt arbitrary even before I knew what the word "arbitrary" meant. I
remember there was this club in the neighborhood next to the

C-Town supermarket called The Crocodile, and on Thursdays in the summer they had a teen night. I begged Mommy to let me go with friends and she wouldn't allow it. I might've been fourteen at the time, very much so a teen, but I still couldn't go. It wasn't because I hadn't done my chores or I was cuttin' up in the streets. It was just always no. Growing up in a West Indian household it often felt like "no" was the default parenting technique. Mommy never explained why I couldn't do stuff; she just said that as her child I couldn't, and I didn't question it. Mommy had me when she was sixteen and would often joke that she soft-pitched *Teen Mom* to MTV producers long before the show took off. She did a great job at hiding the challenges of being a child raising a child, but her fear of me repeating her mistake was so ripe, it robbed me of a lot of experiences. So, when in doubt, she said no.

After receiving my hour of recreation from the warden, I had to find a new way to occupy my time, which is partly how my love for reading began. As firm as my mom was about who I spent time with, she never questioned why I was reading books written by R. L. Stine, Eric Jerome Dickey, or even Zane. I had a vivid imagination, so whatever was on the page in the book I was reading, I could picture in my mind. This made not being allowed to go outside often a little more bearable. While all my other friends were living their real lives, I was in the crib reading and going wherever the characters went. Once I got older, Mommy loosened the leash a bit and I began to gallivant all over the city with friends. I didn't question why more freedom had been given. I was just happy about it. Maybe Mommy finally realized I wasn't buggin' when I was outside all those years. Either way, she wasn't saying no, and internally I was saying "Hell, yes!"

I might've been seventeen the first time my friends and I went to Times Square by ourselves. It was just Times Square, but, in our heads, we were grown. There's something about New York City that's exciting and electrifying, and that feeling intensifies at night. My friends and I were high school seniors, so not only were we about to graduate, but we also had matriculated out of our Converses and Jordans and began wearing heels. Learning how to walk in pumps is one thing; learning how to walk a New York City block in three-inch heels is an Olympic sport, one our good knees and youthful ankles were able to withstand. Jeans that were once a little baggy were now figure-flattering, and V-neck tees and blouses exposing cleavage that had no business being exposed were among some of our fashion choices. I didn't have much of a butt (more on this in a subsequent chapter) so I worked with what I did have, which was a taut tummy. I was known to flaunt my midriff once I was safely out of Queens and far enough away from my mother's ability to *boppity-bop-bop* me with a belt if I decided to get fresh. Mommy also let me tend to the scaffolding on my forehead when she finally allowed me to get my eyebrows threaded. Thin eyebrows were a thing growing up. My eyebrows, on the other hand, looked as if I had two packs of Afro Kinky strung across my forehead. Once the beautician finished mowing my brows, I felt like a new person, which did wonders for my confidence. My friends and I were shedding a bit of teenage awkwardness as well. We'd made it through four emotional years of high school—boys, Regents exams, rumors—and that feeling of "We did it!" was enormous for our emotional development as young women and showed up in ways we couldn't articulate but could feel.

Times Square was always crowded and loud, but it felt good to finally be out of the house and experience things in real time with friends instead of hearing about it the day after. Yes, 42nd Street felt like a tourist attraction (because it is), but it was also something to experience and conquer. Being out way past when the streetlights came on felt rebellious and I loved every bit of it. Once, the girls and I made plans for dinner and a movie. By dinner, I'm sure we went to Red Lobster or some other chain restaurant. We may have thought we were budding foodies, but we clearly had the palate range of an aardvark. We laughed, talked about whatever teenage gossip we had going on at the time, and made our individual life plans completely unaware that life laughs at your plans. After eating my weight in Cheddar Bay Biscuits and washing them down with a virgin piña colada, the idea of going to a movie seemed exhausting.

"C'mon y'all. We're gonna be late and I wanna catch the previews," Camille said.

"Aigh't, let me grab my purse," Kimberly replied.

"You guys," I groaned. "Do you really still want to see the movie? It's already dark out and we're going to have to take the train all the way back to Queens."

"Shenequa, you're finally out of the house and you want to go back in! Bring yo ass on and stop being a granny," Camille said.

I would be called a granny by a lot of people—family included—until I was well into my thirties. As a seventeen-year-old with an overprotective mother, I was supposed to want to go out and party at all times of night, but now that I finally had the chance I didn't want to. Maybe I was more driven by my mother's "No, you can't go" than anything else? Maybe I thought I was missing out on something and dinner at Red Lobster in Times Square proved I wasn't missing much. Whatever I assumed would happen while I was out didn't happen. What did take place was something I didn't expect. I never thought I'd be able to go out, much less stay out later than before, but still want to be home earlier than my friends. I'd had my fill. I laughed, contributed to the conversation, and was fully present in that moment.

But now, I was ready to go.

The idea of hopping on the bus to transfer to the 7 train was fine when I was leaving my house at about five or six in the evening. It wasn't so appealing leaving the city at ten or eleven o'clock at night. Uber and Lyft weren't a thing back then, so I had to truck it back home in the dark and the MTA is a real magical place once the sun goes down, like an underfunded version of Hogwarts. My stomach was full, and my burps were now a tangy blend of coconut from the coladas and cheesy garlic from the biscuits. Wearing heels was cute in theory, but now in practice my feet were killing me. I'm almost positive I was wearing some Steve Madden special, which felt like a proper introduction to "womanhood" at the time compared to some of the Payless shoes I used to buy. After wearing them once or twice, the heel would wear down and the small, round, metal stub inside the heel would make a click-clacking sound as I walked by. The night, in my book, had run its course.

"Y'all, I'm sorry, but I can't. I'm too tired," I confessed.

"Tired?! You're tired?! We ain't did nothing," Kimberly said.

"I know, I know," I said sheepishly. "But I want to go home. Y'all have fun, but I'm gonna catch the train."

Tension filled the air. Kimberly, now visibly annoyed, turned to Camille to confirm if she was still down to go to the movies or would she betray the night's agenda and head home as well.

"Okay, Shenequa. Well, get home safe," Camille said.

Kimberly gave me a half-hearted goodbye and began walking toward the theater. As I headed into the station, I was ballooned with guilt. They seemed motivated by the excitement and the possibility of the night. I didn't share that same feeling. I also didn't think I'd get tired so quickly and want to leave. I didn't know wanting to go back home would be considered a friendship felony, but I longed for the comfort of my bed and whichever book I was reading at the time. After being under my mother's thumb for so long, it never occurred to me that once "free" and able to explore, I'd need to adjust to how different actually being outside was. I know it sounds weird, but the downside of not going anywhere as a kid was not being able to go anywhere, but being in the house all the time meant I created comfort and safety by myself. I learned how to find warmth and coziness within me.

Similar situations would routinely occur. "You never want to do anything," Tisha would say, or a "Look at granny, ready to go," from Camille. Whenever I partied, stayed out late, and got drunk there were never any problems, but when I didn't want to be a "team player" and participate, that's when I was accused of being a Debbie Downer. Those moments when I thugged it out and stayed out with the girls were fun, don't get me wrong, but I always remember taking a beat to myself. I'd find a corner or a couch and sit for fifteen or twenty minutes to recharge my social battery. I'm unsure if Kim or Camille understood, but that was my way of surviving the night. Looking back on it, I'm sure I must've looked bananas. Sitting down instead of making my way to the dance floor at the height of the Snoop Dogg and Pharrell "Drop It Like It's Hot" or "Beautiful" era feels like an abomination, but it was either gather my strength or gather my jacket from coat check.

I'm just going to say the one thing I'm not supposed to say that probably gives credence to the whole "granny" title I've earned over the years. "Having fun" is exhausting. I didn't know how to say it then, but "having a good time" in the way people in their twenties are encouraged to is too much. You have to shower, get dressed, do your hair, do your makeup, and after doing your full face, you balloon with pride because it actually came out great only to realize you either forgot to use primer or you tried to draw on a wing only to mess up the whole look.

But wait, we're not done.

During all of this, you realize you haven't been charging your phone and pray to the cellular gods your 20 percent battery life will magically become a full battery in ten minutes. Pre-game at the crib with a drink or two, receive a text from your ex that reads "Hey, do you have time to talk?" which can either mean "I'm sorry for everything. I still love you," or "I just got my lab results back," and *then* you arrive at the club or party. The energy it takes to feel good in the way that you're "supposed" to feel good left me depleted.

A few years later, now post-undergrad, my friends and I moved on from the elementary amusement of Times Square and began frolicking in Manhattan's more trendy neighborhoods, such as the Meatpacking District. This area is where you can scout the next face of Wilhelmina as they jaywalk, dine at a cute restaurant, or take a well-lit photo on the cobblestone streets that end up looking like a *Live. Laugh. Love* stock image. One night after an event, Camille, Kimberly, myself, and another friend, Fiona, drove around for a while trying to find something to get into.

"Do you want to go Pastis?" Fiona said.

"Nah, I'm not hungry," Kimberly responded.

"Aren't they expensive?" I asked.

"How about Brooklyn?" Camille suggested while munching on some potato chips. "I'm sure there's a party in Brooklyn."

"I live in Harlem. I'm not going to Brooklyn," Kimberly said.

"Wanna go to the movies?" I suggested.

The silence in the car let me know my idea wasn't even an option.

Sometimes, nights have no plans or agendas and they organically become some of the best experiences of your life. Other times, you're in a car with your friends trying to figure out "what's the move." After the first ten or fifteen suggestions about how the evening can be best enjoyed, I begin to tap out. In this instance, it had been an hour and, true to form, I was ready to go.

"Well, since we're not going anywhere, can y'all drop me off at the train?" I asked.

"Why do you always want to leave?" Camille said. "What you gonna do at home?"

"Because driving around the Meatpacking District for more than an hour is supposed to be poppin'?" I replied.

"Whatever, Shenequa."

Camille fixed her eyes back on the road and I buried my head in my phone. This moment is small, but it's also layered. There's this unwritten girl code: if the group is out for the night, then you stay with the group, even if nothing substantial comes from the outing. For safety reasons, I get it. But this wasn't that. Camille was driving, and we were all buckled in. Nothing was happening, no plans were solidified, yet I was expected to stay there and do nothing with the group.

Why does girl code dictate that I stay *even when we're doing nothing?* We eventually made our way to Queens and settled at a beer garden in Long Island City. I left shortly after.

I grew tired of the granny moniker I had "earned" simply because I didn't want to go along with the group if the group was staying out or staying out later than I had the energy for. And if I asserted my desire to leave early or not go at all I grew to expect threats. *You're going to wake up one day and regret not having had any fun or memories. You have to live your life!* Translation: You're not doing or participating in the type of fun I want you to have and your refusal to engage makes me sad or question what I'm doing. So, I'm going to guilt you.

I'm well into my thirties now and I'm more upset if I miss out on a JetBlue deal than what party I didn't go to when I was in my twenties. I also didn't want to explain why I would rather be home reading a book than be outside. Yes, I've been drunk. Yes, I've partied. Yes, I stayed out until the sun came up. I've done all those things and if those are the experiences you want to have, Godspeed. They're fun and, depending on how many shots you take, they can be memorable . . . kind of (not really.) But when I'm ready to go, I'm ready to go and I do not feel like explaining why, even if I'm ready to leave fifteen minutes after arriving. Maybe I'm selfish or maybe it's a Gemini thing. One minute we're here for it and then the next we're not, but if I'm not feeling it, I'm simply not feeling it. I began taking stock of how I felt when I was with friends and how I felt when I was alone. With Kim, Cam, and sometimes Fiona, there was always laughter, great conversation, and camaraderie. But when I was alone, I was a bit more relaxed and didn't feel obligated to have the kind of fun that left me depleted. I didn't have to be "on." In 2017, I randomly flew to France. Capital One had foolishly given me a line of credit, so your girl started messing hers up and booking flights. In October of that year, I stayed in Paris for two days and spent my time either staring at the Eiffel Tower or taking walks throughout the city. Then, I hopped on a train to London and sat on a bench and people watched for a few days while chomping on fried dumplings and ackee. I didn't think my plans were boring. I was proud I had gone abroad by myself. More importantly, I loved that I didn't have to explain to anyone why my simple itinerary was divorced of all the tourist-y things. I wanted to chill and see what everyday life in London felt like, and it felt great. Anyone who knows me knows I feel a strange pull to the city of London. Maybe it's because it's the first place I went to on my own. Maybe it's the robust West Indian and West African culture there that I'm attracted to, but for a lot of folks, they can't get past the weather. A lot of my friends were booking flights to sunny Miami. I, on the other hand, was riding the Tube and exploring Shoreditch and Brixton, gray clouds and rainy weather be damned.

I don't know if I would call myself a sad girl, per se, but there is a bit of disenchantment that I've always had, so much so that I feel a tiny sense of relief on gray or cloudy days, which might be why London always felt like a second home. The overcastness validates me while bright and sunny days make me feel as if I'm not justified in feeling blue. Traditional thinking suggests that if the sun's out, it's easier for someone to chase and even catch a bit of joy or happiness. "Go out, get some sun," people say. There is scientific evidence that the sun does help to boost your mood, but for someone like me, a sunny day only reminds me of an emotional goal that feels foreign to me and out of my grasp. Let me be clear: I logically know and emotionally appreciate the beauty of a beautiful day and a clear blue sky. I don't turn my nose up at seventy-five- or eighty-degree weather. But something about a sunny day magnifies the constant disenchantment I feel and the pressure to "have fun" and "be exciting." Grayness, clouds, and even rain feel more like home. A beautiful day is treated as something precious, that shouldn't be wasted. Blue skies, easy sun, and gentle breezes are to be savored. Most importantly, you cannot be sad, or at least that's the expectation. YOU. MUST. BE. HAPPY. Rainy days don't demand such an emotional obligation and, thus, a performance. Rainy days, like my alone time, don't require me to be on.

Flying to Europe unlocked another emotional puzzle piece: whatever mood I was in that day was okay because I was alone, and I wasn't expected to be anything other than who I was at that moment. Whenever you agree to go somewhere or do something with someone, nine times out of ten, you're agreeing to be in an agreeable mood. This isn't explicitly stated, but no one wants to make a Target run with someone who has the personality of a hemorrhoid. I knew early on I couldn't predict what mood I'd be in when it came time to go out, but I knew for the sake of the group, for the sake of the plans, in honor of all the "Girl, what you wearing?" conversations that were had, I HAD to be in a good mood, and I HAD to show up, and I HAD to perform even if I emotionally couldn't.

There's also this idea that the thought of "having fun" should energize you.

"C'mon, girl. I know you worked a full week and you're going through this bad breakup, and your doctor wants to run some more tests to rule out cancer, but it's happy hour. It'll be fun. It'll take your mind off things."

"Fun," "partying," "drinks"—those are supposed to be the great equalizer when life begins to life and it's like, yeah, no. "Having fun" can be exhausting, but that pressure to be in a space you're not in for the sake of the team has never been something I could successfully pull off. Whenever I was alone, that wasn't a hurdle I had to jump over. Me, my clouds, my rainy day, and whatever mood I was in at the time were good enough and didn't require any explanation. I'm always good enough for me when it's just me.

I didn't know it then that who I was (and largely still am) is an introvert. The word hadn't made its way into my lexicon at the time, and I hadn't heard any of my friends use it either. Instead, I thought I was just the "boring" girl or, worse, that there was something socially and emotionally wrong with me. When my friends had the energy and desire to party and go out, I'd quickly hit my wall and want to leave. I didn't know I was just wired differently or, rather, wired quietly.

"I love partying, but I also love being in my house by eight o'clock, too," Nicole said.

Nic, a curly-haired Aquarius from New Orleans, is a friend of mine whom I met while working for a media company. She led the social media department and would regularly polish off a sleeve of double-stuffed Oreos while Hula-Hooping at her desk. No one ever knew where her collection of Hula-Hoops came from (some were glittery, others had sand in them so you could hear a *whoosh* when you used them), but Nic always got her work done, so we ignored her prediabetic Hula-Hoop behavior.

On a slow day at work, Nic made what I thought was a mind-blowing statement. She was able to go out and have fun but also be home at a reasonable hour, like eight or so. I had no idea you could gallivant, laugh, take selfies, drink, dance, and still be in the house before the werewolves came out to play. I was still young in my own adulthood, well into my twenties, and very much felt like I needed permission when it came to my feelings. So, when I heard Nic succinctly explain how I would've preferred to spend recreational time (in the event I wanted to recreate at all), it confirmed that it could be done and that I wasn't abnormal for wanting it done in that way. I don't *have* to stay out all night if I don't want to. I don't *have* to drink all the time. I also don't *have* to indulge in anyone else's definition of fun if it doesn't jive with my own. Being an introvert doesn't mean you don't go out. Being an introvert means that when your social battery gets low, you come back in. And what hurts is that so many people don't or simply choose not to respect introverts. The biggest difference between my friends from high school and me was that they wanted the thrill and excitement that come with being on a roller coaster, whereas I was okay with walking around the carnival and playing a few games. Getting on the roller coaster was cool every now and again, but simply walking around the carnival was kind of lame for them.

Now, as an adult, it's great to no longer be the odd one out simply because I don't want to go out. I have a colleague whose favorite day of the week is Friday and who says her favorite thing to do is sleep. She thinks it's enjoyable, easy, and refreshing and that's how she chooses to spend her free time as a grown person. I don't live for Fridays, per se (Sundays are actually my favorite day of the week), but doing nothing is a hobby of mine that I employ from time to time and I'm thankful more people understand and respect it.

I'm not saying I hate extroverts, but that community largely gives me gas. The older I get, the easier it is for me to identify my tribe, and when it comes to extroverts, I have to keep them at a healthy distance. This muscle was unintentionally strengthened throughout the pandemic. COVID was an extreme case that involved the deaths of more than one million Americans (and countless others globally), but the one upside for me, a self-described introvert, was that I got to stay indoors. When I needed fresh air, I took a walk, but whereas others felt depleted being away from other people, I was the most energized, productive, and emotionally full I'd been in years. Now, a few years removed from the worst of the pandemic, I'm beginning to see there are more like-minded folks. There's a community of adults thirty-three and older who all have their bonnets or durags on by eight and are in bed, under the covers, scrolling through social media until God knows when.

I've waited a long time to finally be among the general population who traffics their joy and social life between noon and 6 p.m. (Hours of operation are subject to change during daylight savings.) I'm now part of a group of people who know grocery shopping is a legitimate activity, just like walking through Target is live-action Pinterest board building. So, now when someone asks, "How was your weekend?" and I say, "I bought groceries," that person knows I participated in an activity, and I did something with my life.

For me, being in your twenties and not wanting to stay out until dawn every weekend meant you were corny. Being in your thirties and staying out after dark to party can be viewed as a cry for help. Gone are open bars and in their place are baby showers. Walking around 42nd Street in heels used to be a breeze. Now walking up a flight of stairs can feel like you're carrying a Pottery Barn sectional. Yes, this is a result of getting older, but it's also finally become cool and almost acceptable to slow down.

I can't remember exactly when the slowdown happened but I'm thankful for it. There used to be a time when I could take three or four shots and still function. Now, if I drink a hard seltzer, I have to text with one eye open just to ensure my *they're*, *there*, and *their* are all correct. Yes, people get older, things and palates hopefully change, but I'm so happy that the "granny" in me that was always clowned for wanting to be in her bed earlier than others can finally flourish.

Grandma Shenequa has made it to the other side victorious.

10

Lowered Expectations

I remember the exact moment I became team Winston. I was in my mid-twenties when my cousin Tara invited me to her Connecticut home for a Halloween party. To prepare, I helped put up decorations of skeletons, witches, and faux headstones, while Winston, her then live-in boyfriend and now husband, filled jack-o'-lanterns with candy. There were several pots on top of the stove with food also baking in the oven. Tara, keeping an eye on everything, also made a spiked green punch for the dozen or so friends and family she invited. But as the evening wore on, people started to flake. A lot of "Sorry, I can't make it" or "Something just popped up" flooded her text messages. Eventually, what should've been a proper bashment instead became an evening at the crib for me, Tara, and Win.

Tara wore a makeshift Superwoman costume. She threw on a raggedy shoulder-length black wig and placed a plastic golden tiara on top. I, despite my best efforts, didn't have a costume. No matter how much I try, I'm rarely prepared for the holiday even though it's the same day every year. At the end of September going into October, I always promise myself to dress up and do it big for Halloween. One year, I even decided I would be global warming. (I figured if I walked around wearing a blow-up globe with me wrapped in a blanket, people would get it. Bad execution but you understand the idea.) But as the month goes on, I always forget, which renders me costume-less. So, I went rummaging through Tara's closet and found a cheap black top hat and another shoulder-length black curly wig. (Tara has a lot of wigs.) I threw on some big bug-eye black shades and used a broom as my fake guitar and decided to be Slash from Guns N' Roses. Out of righteous retaliation for everyone who didn't show up, Tara and I danced all night. We blasted Michael Jackson's *Thriller* and performed the iconic zombie choreography from the video. According to Winston, in between my carrying on and Tara's own brand of foolishness, I tried to leave the house in the dead of night to take the MetroNorth back to the city. Thank God, he stopped me because supposedly I was on the move.

As the night wore on, and the green punch caught up with me, I passed out on the living room couch while Winston took Tara upstairs to bed. Sometime in the middle of the night, I made my way to the guest room to continue my Tequila-induced slumber. The next morning, Tara and I woke up around the same time and recounted the craziness of the night before as best as our foggy memories would allow. We both looked like we had fifty dollars' worth of well-packed Trader Joe's grocery bags under our eyes, but the laughs and good times were worth it. As we walked downstairs, I was ready to roll up my sleeves and help Tara with the dishes. We were too drunk to be responsible and clean up last night, so I was certain we'd pay for it now. As we made our way to the kitchen, I was shocked to find that it wasn't dirty at all. In fact, it was spotless.

The food was packed in plastic Tupperware containers and stored in the refrigerator with a Tetris-like precision. The smell of lemon-scented Clorox tickled my nose. Aluminum foil pans were thrown away, and the trash was taken out. The utensils used to prepare the food along with all the dirty dishes were washed, dried, and stored in their proper cabinets. The counters sparkled and the floor was swept. The kitchen, formally ground zero for the party that never happened, was now pristine.

"Wassup, Chin Chin?" Winston said. His scratchy baritone filled the room. "Hey, baby," he said before kissing Tara.

As Tara slid-walked in her fuzzy socks across the cherry hardwood floor to the stove, her robe dragging behind her, I stood in the middle of the living room in amazement, my palm cupping my face in pure shock. Just a few hours ago, their apartment had been transformed into a spooky den for a Halloween festivity (they even bought a smoke machine) and now it was a clean-living space. Winston had done something that none of the men I'd dated had ever done. He'd noted that his girlfriend had decorated and cooked the night before and chose to clean up while she slept. This was the first time I had seen equality up close and in real life.

"Chin!" Tara said breaking me out of my bewilderment. "Earth to Chin! Want some coffee?"

All three of us sat on their charcoal-colored couch while Winston gave Tara and me a play-by-play of our drunken escapades. Our conversation weaved in and out of the silly to the serious. At one point, Tara got on her soapbox and started telling me all about her 9/11 conspiracy theories.

"I just want to know what happened to the third building. Someone tell me what happened to the third building," Tara protested.

"What third building are you even talking about?" I questioned.

"Exactly. What third building?" she said.

Winston broke up all the federal government cover-up conversation when he told us about an old high school buddy of his who'd had a robust Facebook following at the time despite possibly having a warrant out for his arrest. It was, for all intents and purposes, a lively couch convo.

"Ah, man," Winston said in an exaggerated, singsong fashion. "I think I'm getting hungry now."

Tara then pulled back the blanket she and I were sharing and said: "Guess it's my turn." She walked into the kitchen and began taking out the neatly packed Tupperware Winston had put away the night before to heat up some food and make him a plate. Now under different circumstances, my inner Roxane Gay would've come roaring to the forefront reminding my cousin and any woman that her value as a person shouldn't be determined by her service to a man. With Destiny's Child "Independent Women" playing ever so softly in the background for dramatic effect, I would stand high and mighty on the shoulders of every feminist and womanist before me and remind Tara that Winston is grown, and if *he* is hungry then *he* can go into the fridge and feed himself. Oddly enough, that didn't happen. Instead, what I saw Tara do was continue the thread that's an apparent connective tissue throughout their relationship. Seeing how Winston helped Tara and then Tara helped Winston was foreign to me but also astonishing to see.

I grew up on Oceania Street in Bayside, Queens. My Jamaican home was a revolving door for extended family and friends who after immigrating from *yahd* needed a place to lay their head and get their bearings. My house was composed of my mom, my grandmother, my aunt Lavern, my older cousin Tisha, and her brother, Andre, whom we all called by his middle name, Ian (pronounced EEEE-yon. You've got to elongate the o-n part, to give it the necessary Jamaican lilt). It was a three bedroom, one-and-a-half bath with a full basement. The bedrooms and full bathroom were upstairs, but I mostly stayed in the basement because I could watch all the cartoons and music videos I wanted and not have to fight anyone for the remote. We had a bright-yellow awning, which over time, looked more mustard, and every spring, the tree in the front would explode with delicate pink cherry blossoms. It was my responsibility to clean up all the fallen leaves, and later when Tara came to live with us, she had to grab a broom and garbage bag too. Mommy loved the tree, despite the allergies it caused her. She always marveled at its personality, the way one branch would curve to the left or how another would stand straight up.

Life on Oceania Street was memorable, and it was also where the first seeds of independence were planted and watered. I must've been seven or eight when a mattress Auntie Lavern ordered arrived at the house. Now, maybe Auntie didn't pay the extra money to have the delivery guys bring the mattress upstairs to her room, and I don't know where Ian was, but I remember it was an all-out team effort for the women in the house. Mommy, my grandmother, Lavern, Tisha, and my scrawny little arms dragged the mattress through the narrow front door, past the kitchen opening, pivoting slightly to the right where the stairs were. Me, Mommy, and Grandma had to push, while Tisha, just a few stairs ahead (and frankly squeezed into a corner), shoved in an upward motion, and Auntie Lavern at the top of the staircase pulled. Eventually, we got enough of the mattress up enough of the stairs to where we could flip it over the railing. There was more pushing and pulling and heavy breathing to get into Auntie's bedroom, but the brunt of the work had been done. Exhausted but proud of what we accomplished, I remember thinking to myself, "We didn't need those guys anyway."

I grew up seeing Black women do hard things, like lift a mattress up a flight of stairs or raise children by themselves. I've also seen Black women do necessary things like clean a kitchen. I rarely saw a man, much less a Black man, help with heavy things or do household chores. It's so ingrained in me to do things myself, I'm almost shocked *if* a man offers to help. On a flight back from LA recently, I lifted my carry-on into an overhead bin only to realize it didn't fit. Trying once more, a man stopped and asked if he could assist. Without thinking, I said no thank you.

Seeing men assist, in any capacity, wasn't prevalent growing up on Oceania Street, which made Winston's act of partnership so huge. It wasn't just about the dishes, just like it wasn't just about the mattress.

. . .

I've always believed men and women were equal, and for a long time, I thought everyone else felt the same. That all changed one Thursday night when I watched a particular episode of *Martin*. In the '90s, Fox's prime-time television lineup was undefeated. It was *Martin* at 8 p.m., then *Living Single* at 8:30, followed by *New York Undercover* at 9 p.m. Before Shonda Rhimes owned and invented Thursdays with *Grey's Anatomy*, *Scandal*, and *How to Get Away with Murder*, all '90s kids were tuned in to Fox on Thursday nights.

It's easy to look back on *Martin* and turn your nose up at the obvious chauvinism, but even as a little girl something about Martin Payne didn't sit right with me. In one particular episode, Tommy, Pam, Cole, and Gina are all at Martin's house when the topic of money comes up.[1] Martin and Tommy agree that money is power, and as the night continues, Martin questions Gina about why she gave Cole twenty-five dollars. Gina explains she needed money for a cab one day and since he was busy at the time, she borrowed the money from Cole instead. After learning this, Martin throws a fit. He conjures up an absurd story alleging that *his* woman borrowing money from another man is disrespectful because that man now has "power" over her. It's then that Pam, Martin's archenemy, drops the hammer on Martin's ego to inform him Gina's the one with all the power because she makes significantly more money than he does.

As a kid, I remember watching that episode unsure of why there was an issue at all. Why would a man be upset if his girlfriend or wife had a larger income than he did? I also couldn't figure out why Tisha Campbell's character felt the need to keep this information from Martin. What did she have to be ashamed of? She had a job, right? And she earned her money, yes? If men allegedly don't want gold diggers, then the logical desire should be a woman who has her own gold, no? Why was money, specifically a woman with lots of money, such a touchy subject? It all seemed so odd to me. What I didn't know was that despite *Martin* being a scripted comedy, this episode also expressed an unwritten rule in the real world: women are to pretend that the men in our lives are Superman even though most of us are wearing the cape.

But, as the years continued and as my desire to be desired by boys increased, I slowly fell into misogyny's grip. At home, Mommy, Grandma, and Auntie Lavern ran the world. They also let me be my quirky, random, and reclusive self. It was only when I was outside that I saw a woman's strength or leadership wasn't something boys admired. As I got older, I noticed the way boys treated the girls they liked and how it differed greatly from their treatment of girls they didn't like. I wanted to be liked, so I thought if I agreed with boys and their opinions then they'd dig me more, even if their language of

girls and women was acidic, their points of view were illogi-
cal, and their beliefs were rooted in feminine deterioration and
dehumanization.

My father not being around didn't help shape my view of
what kind of guy I *should* be attracted to, or what behavior I
should accept. It deepened a longing for attention, tenderness,
and care from men. So, as it pertained to boys, I was on my
own to figure it all out. I never heard my father speak tenderly
to my mom or see him buy her flowers. Conversely, I also never
heard him use harsh language with her. The only advice I ever
received from my mom about dating was "Don't come home
pregnant," which really helps you secure clients when you're
in the marketplace, so to speak. I wasn't bold enough to go to
third base or anything (you know, fingers below the belt), but
I still wanted to be wanted by all the cuties in school and the
ones from round the way. Something about a boy liking me
gave me a value and confidence I didn't know how to articulate
but I knew I wanted to experience often.

I still cringed whenever guys freely substituted a girl's name
with the word "bitch," as if saying her name, whoever she was,
was such a laborious task. It was never *"Shorty with the curly
hair"* or *"The one who was standing next to whasshername from
English. She had on the white and black 11s."* Normal descrip-
tors were too burdensome. It was always *"That bitch with the
wavy hair."* I ignored the hurtful language because speaking up
would mean losing what little interest these boys were paying
me, and, sadly, they weren't calling me a bitch, so I assumed
I was immune to their corrosive tongues. While I could easily see when racism was at play because the big bad wolf was
usually someone outside of the community, and oftentimes
someone in a uniform, it took a while for me to realize when
misogynoir was a factor.

A chasm, however, between wanting a man's attention and affection and my own self-worth began to form when I became the victim of unwanted catcalls. Now, at about sixteen or seventeen, with a noticeable C cup and shapely legs, the attention that was once paid to whichever elder woman who held my hand as we walked down the block was now focused solely on me as I walked alone. And what I previously assumed was a man's sincere inability to control himself when a beautiful woman was in the vicinity started to look a lot more like sport.

Men, often three or four at a time, would stand on the corner and whisper among themselves as I approached as if a game plan was being devised. As I walked past, the quarterback among the crew would fire off whatever comment they assumed would merit the most laughter between their fellow brethren. The goal was never to get my phone number or even get me to smile back at them. Instead, it was to earn the respect and admiration of another man at my expense and comfort. As I got older, I became the recipient of several "Dumbass bitch!" insults or my personal favorite: "You not even that bad, shorty! Fuck you being so stush for?" It would be too easy to say I was hurt after I was accosted by men on the street. This moral one-eighty I was experiencing was deeper than that because I realized these small interactions were just transactions for them. The faux attention and in some instances "kindness" were their down payment to me. I was supposed to "pay them back" with anything from a smile that proved I acquiesced to the moment or a licking of my lips coupled with a "meet me at this address in thirty minutes" kind of deal. And when neither one of those things happened, my potential services were no longer needed, and neither was "respecting" me. I wish men knew that they could successfully get to manhood without disrespecting or hurting women in the process.

. . .

In my experience, I've learned that depending on a man, whether for emotional parental support, to lift a mattress, or to clean a dirty kitchen is a fool's errand. Yes, Tara and I could've washed the dishes. In fact, it didn't even occur to me that the responsibility of cleaning the kitchen was anyone else's job but mine and Tara's. And if we didn't want to bust some suds, then my dating experiences with a lot of men has shown me the kitchen would've remained dirty. And it was this instance, before ever knowing what a love language was, that made me realize actually doing things in service to me and for us is *my* thing. Managing chores around the house or taking care of things that both of us need or can benefit from feels like care and attention. I can do complicated or difficult things on my own. There was once a time when I had to reduce fractions, but to have a partner who helps makes things easier without me having to *tell him* gives me the room to feel more emotions and not just be a "strong Black woman." No other race of women has their strength weaponized against them the way Black women do. Just because we can do hard things doesn't give everyone else license to leave the hard things up to us.

And when you're as fiercely independent as I've been conditioned to be, it creates a double-edged emotional sword. On the one hand, I have historical evidence that proves depending on myself yields positive results. But on the other side, it means my to-do list is nonstop and the deep sigh of relief that can only come from a helping hand is something I do not experience. True partnership and aid would mean I have an opportunity to relax and to just be. So much of a Black woman's identity circles around how much she can do for others. If there were more resources for women, especially Black women, we could explore who we are and play with our newly

discovered emotional identities, instead of having to be everyone else's safety net.

. . .

Winston and Tara have been married for nine years. They've
graduated from their two-bedroom townhome and moved into
a three-bedroom rancher. They've got a sunroom, a mudroom,
a fully stocked pantry, and an extra refrigerator, which in my
opinion, is the truest sign of wealth and prosperity in America.
At family gatherings, I often see Winston standing against a
far wall chattin' someone up while Tara's in the kitchen pre-
paring Winston's plate. She always makes Winston a plate and
every time I see it, I'm never appalled. I just think back to the
time Winston cleaned up the kitchen for Halloween, or when
he nearly had a heart attack after receiving the bill at STK in
the Meatpacking District for Tara's thirtieth birthday party.
(It was like eight of us in a private room. I'm sure he's still
paying down the interest.) Or the countless times Tara had to
leave a family dinner early to work the night shift and Winston packed her dinner in some Tupperware and cleaned up
the kitchen while still entertaining guests. Seeing that healthy
display of fifty-fifty was not only heartwarming and hopeful,
but it did something to me.

Their partnership softened me in ways I didn't expect or
know could even happen. This more tender side made me realize I'd be more inclined to cook for a man if I knew I didn't
have to tell him to wash the dishes. I'd be more willing to rub
a man's back if I saw him work hard to provide a safe and stable
home for us, and I'd be happy to do for him if I saw that he
was also happy to do for me. If men romantically, emotionally,
and mentally poured into me as much as I was *expected* to pour
into them, maybe I would have better experiences. Many men
have fancied the idea of controlling me instead of being kind

to me. They wanted power not knowing or, rather, not caring to know that if they treated me with respect, tenderness, and love, they'd probably get whatever they asked for. I'd likely even make them a plate. But they didn't want Shenequa to lovingly do for them; they wanted to command Shenequa to make them a plate. I look back on a lot of the relationships I have been in and wonder if those guys ever really loved me, or did they simply love me loving them?

To see Winston care for my cousin was (and is) great, but his simple act of washing the dishes also inspired me to dedicate an entire chapter in my book to their relationship, which seems weird, but if you think about it, it's also sad as all get-out. Is the bar so low for me (and maybe other heterosexual women) that I'm willing to praise a man for taking on a single household chore? Winston didn't build a house or stop an active shooter. He washed dishes! Is that really all it takes for me to become Mrs. Fix-a-Man-a-Plate? Apparently!

Partnership, true partnership that involves give and take, was something I always believed was the right way a relationship should function, but I never saw or experienced it. And when I witnessed it with Tara and Win, I felt both vindicated and saddened. I knew what I required from men wasn't a lot. I wasn't asking these men to fly me to the Amalfi Coast (in 2019, I took myself because that's what you do when you have unlimited PTO) or buy me a fancy watch (when I got my advance, I also bought myself a Movado). I just didn't want to carry the entire relationship on my shoulders. Yet it left me with deep sorrow that even the little I was asking for, the literal crumbs, I couldn't receive. Tara has always been a little more chill than I am. She doesn't have an easy life, per se, but there is a level of ease she carries that I don't. Maybe it's because I'm a type A person and she's a mellow Cancer, but one of the key differences in our demeanor is that Tara also has the loving support of a husband she knows she can depend on. Tara doesn't have to do it alone; she has Win who can ride shotgun with her to Target or to dinner or wherever. That security and love shows up in Tara's life and on her skin in a way that I can see in her because it's not something I have in me. The love between Tara and Winston can be likened to a safety net. They have each other and can lean on one another to be strong. I can't pinpoint what it is about me, but I tend to attract "fragile" men who see my strength and then show their "appreciation" by throwing all their emotional woes on me with the belief I'm supposed to solve their problems. Why? Well, because I'm a "strong Black woman" who can allegedly handle it. That's why.

. . .

Tara and Win don't know I look at them as #Relationship-Goals. They're so in sync, it's a force to witness. Once, I went to their house for a visit and we went bowling. (Tara won, I think.) When we pulled back up to the house, they both got out of the car and each one, without saying it to the other, began pulling up weeds on opposite sides of the house. (Nah, I think Winston won.) There was no prior discussion about hiring a gardener or anything like that. They both just saw the weeds and, instinctively, Tara went to the right side of the house and Winston took the left side. I stood outside of the car and watched them both take care of their house because they looked at their home as a mutual responsibility. Whenever I'm around them, it's love and laughs between them, which lets me know that when both people are doing their part, it's a joy to actually be in the relationship. Winston isn't always expected to wash the dishes and Tara isn't always required to cook. They're both supposed to do what needs to be done to make their union work. My cousin is a much better person because of Win. He waters and protects her, and I hope she does the same for him, not just because she's my cousin but because it's the right thing to do.

And guess what? Now they have a dishwasher.

11

BBL

I was born with a bit of an issue.

I don't speak about it often because it hasn't stunted my ability to lead a full and successful life, but growing up there were a lot of tear-filled "why me?" moments. Mommy was supportive, always patiently listening to me as I repeatedly questioned why I couldn't be like everyone else I knew or saw. She'd give me a hug and kiss, tell me I was just as beautiful, and try to remind me we're all unique in our own special way. I look back at those instances and wonder how Mommy put up with my constant sadness as I threw this issue on her day after day, year after year. But then again, Mommy didn't have this dilemma. She wasn't born with my problem, and she didn't have to experience its stinging pains and disappointments. Mommy had no idea what it was like being a Black girl with a flat ass.

Growing up in a household with full-figured Jamaican women, my definition of physical beauty was shaped long before my own figure kicked in. Mommy, standing at a cute five-foot-three, has always had a nice bum. My aunt Lavern, who's a little taller, also had some cushion. My cousin Tisha didn't have a studio apartment hanging behind her, but if she gained a few pounds, she rounded out. Even Tiny B, my grandmother, had a nice high peach.

Me? Yeah, no. It was long-back Lorraine over here.

There are different kinds of asses to admire. There's the high-round butt, which gets a lot of attention for its button-like quality. Then there's the slightly wider, more hip-oriented booty, which doesn't have as much meat but still falls within the figure-eight boundary line. The crème de la crème of all behinds is the badunkadunk. This is the Optimus Prime of booties because it can't get any bigger or better than this. Sometimes the badunkadunk owner chooses to hide said asset, think Barack and Michelle Obama's 2016 *Essence* magazine shoot. The gorgeous presidential couple were on their way out of the White House, but before leaving, they gave the internet more #RelationshipGoals to aspire to by way of beautiful photos. They also had a lot of Americans tastefully choosing their words as many acknowledged that our First Lady was working with a little more back there than we originally thought. But not all licensed badunkadunkers take the Michelle Obama approach. Some want you to know they're God's favorite. So, in the dead of winter, when everyone else is giving the drugstore version of A$AP Rocky and Rihanna at the 2021 Met Gala, here walks in the badunkadunker wearing skin-tight jeggings and a cropped puffer jacket with faux fur around the hood because "It's not that cold outside."

Really, sis?

My family never shamed me or made fun of my athletic build. I was always praised for my height and lean physique. But to turn every corner in my three-bedroom home on Oceania Street and see shapely women didn't do much for my confidence. This feeling also echoed when I was with my two high school friends, Kimberly and Camille, who often made heads turn whenever they walked by. Kim and Cam knew how much I hated my flat ass, so, whenever I was in one of my moods, they'd focus their praise on my toned legs or taut tummy. Seeing voluptuous women in my family, in late '90s and early 2000s hip-hop music videos, and among my friends caused a mental distortion for me. The beauty I saw around me and what was reflected in the mirror didn't align and, because of it, I measured my body against every other woman's and gave myself an F. Because all the women I loved and admired were full-figured, in my mind, the curve of a woman's bum added to her femininity and allure. A woman with a little meat on her bones appeared more captivating, like she had more equity in her womanhood than I did. Take for instance the "traditional" Black girl picture a lot of girls in the '90s took. A group of Black girls, about four, no more than six, may get together and decide to memorialize the moment. After several poses, someone will suggest "the look back at it" stance in which everyone's back is toward the camera so the person viewing the photo will focus on everyone's butt. This picture and moment were not something I ever wanted to participate in. In order to give off the illusion I had a fatty, I had to either poke my butt out, planting seeds for future lower-back problems, or step back with my right leg and place all my body weight on my left side. This incorrect back lunge, if you will, was the only way I could fake any kind of roundness in my rear. Not being part of the big booty brigade plucked at me for a very, *very* long time. And here's the thing, not having a big butt is totally different from not having a behind at all. There are some women who have just enough for their shape. I didn't even have that, which only made my insecurity worse. Things became too much to bear when white women started getting bigger behinds. It was one thing for this problem to be self-contained within the Black community, but when white women started filling out, I was fully prepared to be cremated alive. First, they had privilege and all the fun that comes with it, now they were getting asses too! Immediately no. There used to be a time when if you told a white woman she had a big derriere she would cry. A big butt used to be offensive. Now, white women at the very least understand that having an ass isn't grounds for asking to speak to the manager.

I opened this chapter alleging I was born with an issue, when in all actuality I was a healthy eight-pound baby girl. But not having a big ass felt like I was missing out on something that would've improved my quality of life, and this perspective couldn't be further from the truth. All my life my body has been my first line of defense against everything from cold and flu season to Mommy's belt. My body functions as designed and has never failed me, yet I didn't appreciate it because my ass muscles weren't big, which if you think about it, is ass-backward. (Ba-dum-tss! See what I did there?)

As far as butts are concerned, mine worked. Every time I sat down, there it was, reporting for ass duty, absorbing the gentle impact of sitting, and also helping me to do whatever butts are meant to help you do. But for years, I spoke in a cruel manner to my body because it didn't mirror the ones I thought were valuable and desirable. Could you imagine if every mean thing we said to our bodies resulted in a life-threatening medical issue? Tell your body it's ugly and here's kidney failure. Say you look like an ogre and now you have stage 19 diabetes. Point out that you have six rolls and not a six pack of washboard abs and it's straight to hospice. I was so focused on what I didn't have, that I couldn't even see that my body, as imperfect as it may be, was just right. It would be a while before I could say my body was beautiful and really mean it, but accepting my body for exactly what it was felt okay. My body wasn't doing anything to stop me from loving myself. My inability to get my head out of my own ass is what was holding me back.

Not having a big butt ignited something sour inside of me. I knew I was an attractive girl, but I wasn't content with *just* having a cute face. I wanted the *bawdy* to go with it, which watered the seeds of jealousy inside me. Jealousy is a common emotion but also useless because you're the one doing all the work. Jealousy causes you to tell a story about the other person's "accomplishments" and, in my case, the other woman's rear end. I would spin this tale about how lavish her world supposedly was simply because she had more poking out from behind her. You, the one ballooned with jealousy, shine an unsubstantiated light on the other person and nothing they say or do can undo the narrative you've created in your head. Yet underneath the jealousy is true admiration wrapped in sandpaper that scrapes against your ego. What keeps you connected isn't your own storytelling about the other person's alleged amazing life but the curiosity that comes with imagining what it'd be like to have what you covet.

In my warped mind, women who had bigger behinds were better than me. Women with nice behinds had confidence. They'd have their choice of suitors while dazzling the ones they left out to dry. Their red lipstick would be applied perfectly; they would always smell good, or smell like whatever Rihanna wears because I'm sure she smells amazing. They'd have an excellent credit score, perfectly manicured nails, and clear skin. I was committed to this narrative that you could have a perfect life if you had a big ass. This all sounds ridiculous, I'm aware of that now, but insecurities, especially ones about your body, grab ahold of you and feed you sweet lies that keep you insecure.

Things began to shift for me the summer going into my sophomore year at Hampton University. I physically started to fill out in other areas, which helped me appreciate more of my total package. My broad shoulders made my waist look smaller than it was. My C cups and my moderately sized hips helped me realize I didn't look so bad in the mirror after all. I was about nineteen or twenty, so the back fat and arm jiggle hadn't magically appeared yet, but for the first time I could take a step back and really dig what I was seeing. I used to think my bum was as useless as the letter p in the word raspberry, but over that one summer, I gave myself and my body a little more credit. I was able to do this not only because of how I was developing but also because of my ability to commend other women on their bodies. Recognizing the beauty in another woman who didn't have a huge wagon wasn't difficult for me, and besides, having no ass and being a mean girl would've been doing the absolute most. My insecurity placed me in a vacuum of sorts where only shapely women were in my line of sight. The best example I can give is if your mother drives a red Honda Accord. You know there are other cars on the road, but subconsciously you now only see red Honda Accords. I knew not all women had the figure-eight shape; I just happened to only see the ones who did, and every time I saw a woman with a beautiful backside, I beat myself up for not having one. But while I was filling out in college, I not only began to recognize my own beauty; I also saw the beauty and diversity in different body types. I noticed there were more than just red Honda Accords driving about, if you will. So, "Yeah, she doesn't have a bubble butt, but look at how gorgeous her smile is," or "That short haircut on her accentuates her cheekbones. She's stunning!" I could appreciate another woman's hair, eyes, her smooth skin, the way she carried herself, and her overall aura and still find her beautiful. I finally realized that a woman can be sexy and feminine for myriad reasons, not just because of how round her onion is, and coming to this realization helped boost my own self-esteem.

The pinnacle of acceptance regarding my ass-tronomical issue (I've got jokes all day, folks) came via my college roommate Dominique. Senior year, Domie and I were on Hampton's campus inside Buckman Hall. Right before our respective classes began, some random chick, I can't remember her name, commented on her not-so-big butt, to which Domie brilliantly replied: "Yeah, but I like me, so it's okay." I don't remember who that person was or why they felt the need to objectify Domie and be so loud about it, but we can chalk that up to internalized misogyny never taking any days off. I remember that day vividly. Domie wore light-blue jeans, carried a black tote bag with a brown leather handle, and her mid-length black hair was flat-ironed straight with a part down the middle. Domie, with a smile on her face and her satellite dish-sized dimples on full display, was able to do something I'd struggled with *for years*. She took note of herself in a way that wasn't belittling to others and also accepting of who she was.

Yeah, but I like me, so it's okay.

Hampton University, affectionately referred to as "Our home by the sea," the first and the *real* HU (don't let anyone from Howard University try to brainwash you), is known for many things, including its gorgeous 314-acre campus. Settled between the Virginia Peninsula and the tip of the Chesapeake Bay, HU is also home to some of the country's most beautiful and dynamic Black women. Dark-skinned, light-skinned, curly hair, straight hair, 4C hair, no hair, hazel eyes, brown eyes, four-eyes by way of some dope Warby Parker frames. It doesn't matter, if you're looking for a gorgeous and educated

Black woman, visit Hampton University's campus. Some of the women on campus during my four years at HU were shapely, some were athletic, some were chubby, and all were stunning. Did Domie and her regular-size backside seem to care about her bum only being regular sized? Apparently not. Her empowering words glowed in my head like a neon green sign in the window of a tattoo shop. Domie liked herself despite not having the "all" I foolishly assumed women should possess to be considered desirable. And let's be clear, Domie is *hella* fine, which is why this concept and admission was such a eureka moment for me. Her declaration to love her entire body made it okay for me to accept and respect my own.

It had been about ten years since that transformative moment with Domie inside Buckman Hall. Since that time, social media went from being a thing you paid attention to after school to now having your full attention during all hours of the day. Since that moment, accepting my body became a continuous practice for me that I often struggled with. Yet on the days when I felt like I had made progress, my confidence would take a tumble whenever I went on Instagram or Twitter. I'd see a photo of Angela Bassett right as I'm eating a doughnut and boom! An unexpected jab. Ms. Bassett's diet and exercise regimen are well documented, so it's not judgment I feel when Angela Bassett and her fine self comes across my timeline. What I feel is a loud reminder to be easy when it comes to baked goods. But it's not about Angela Bassett, clearly. It felt like all of sudden everyone became perfect, and being bombarded with all these "perfect women" and their "perfect bodies" on social media felt like I was being emotionally jumped.

And as the meteoric rise of social media continued, gluteal enhancements, known as Brazilian butt lifts, became a thing. When I was growing up in the '90s, if a celebrity wanted to get some work done, they would do their procedure quietly and then show up on a red carpet six or eight weeks later with a new nose or an entirely new face. Then we, the public, would obediently nod our head, silently acknowledging the obvious whilst never verbally calling attention to it. Now, plastic surgery and access to beauty enhancements aren't solely for the rich and famous. You can be a part-time bartender or the most prominent TikTok Tupperware influencer. If you want to surgically alter your body, not only can you do it, but you don't have to be quiet about it. You can get your breasts enhanced and stream the entire ordeal on Instagram Live if you desire. (Leaving the name and social media handle of the surgeon in the caption or comments is considered good internet etiquette.)

On the high end, BBLs can cost a little more than ten thousand dollars. The procedure consists of sucking the fat from one part of your body and then inserting it into your behind. According to the 2020 Aesthetic Plastic Surgery National Databank, there were 40,320 butt augmentations the year most of us were sitting on our ass.[1] All these butt enhancements totaled more than $140 million. Folks were spending big bucks on getting a bigger ass, and if they had the financial means to do so, why not? As a teen and later young adult, I had to make do with not having a butt. Now if you want an ass, you can go buy one. You can go to Target and grab some Talenti gelato and then swing by the doctor's office and grab you a whole new behind. Yet, despite its popularity, BBLs are also one of the most dangerous cosmetic procedures to have done simply because your rear has several large veins, one of which goes directly to your heart. A long metal tube, called a cannula, is used to inject the fat into the buttocks, but some doctors have mistakenly injected fat in the wrong place, which then fast-tracks directly to the heart or lungs, prohibiting blood flow and causing death.[2]

I've always wanted a nice butt. Always! In my fantasy with my big booty, it's a sunny spring day and I'd walk down the street, maybe Tompkins Avenue or Quincy Street in Brooklyn, with my hair in a ponytail, wearing a white tank, a black leather jacket, acid-wash jeans, and heels. Think Beyoncé in her "Diva" video. I'd see a group of guys a few feet away and as I got closer, they would spot me, and their entire conversation would dip to a whisper. And then the really cute one, the Method Man out of the group, would make eye contact with me and I'd look back at him. As me and my booty sashayed down the block (I feel like my fantasy booty should have a name. Let's call her Brenda.) with the spring breeze ruffling the tree leaves, somebody would drive by blasting Amerie's "Why Don't We Fall in Love." These dudes would see me and Brenda and drool, but the Method Man look-alike would be caught up in the rapture just like Anita Baker said, and he and I would be in the rapture just raptured up together! They'd all wipe their mouths and one by one shout a cacophony of respectful and feminist-leaning compliments at me using language that evoked equality and awareness of their male privilege, along with the desire to do their part to destroy the patriarchy. ("Yo, the way Republican senator Tom Cotton used his white male privilege while talking to Judge Ketanji Brown Jackson during her confirmation hearing—I definitely wasn't feeling that!") I'd keep walking down the block, wind blowing in my locs, shooting Meth a sexy wink or whatever. Amerie would fade into the distance. They'd still be thinking about me and Brenda, and for that moment, I'd be that fly girl.

But that fantasy was never going to happen, I mean, maybe the Amerie part, but the drooling over my ass wouldn't take place because that's not *my* body. But when I learned about BBLs, I knew that was the line I wouldn't cross. A new butt isn't the same as applying false lashes, wearing a bodysuit underneath a dress, throwing on a cute wig, or applying a red lip. Those cosmetic choices can be easily reversed by getting undressed or using a makeup wipe. But literally putting my ass on the line wasn't for me. And it was in that moment I realized I was maybe more okay with my body than I knew. I was in my late twenties, maybe knocking on thirty's door, when all of this came together. It was weird because I finally had a chance to get the ass I always wanted. I'd have to save up the money, of course, but I instead chose to rock with what I already had. In photos on social media, a lot of women with enhanced behinds look great. The lighting isn't too harsh, their hair is shiny and full, the contour and blush placement is correct. Their eye shadow is well-blended (sometimes there's even a little cut-crease action happening) and the lip gloss is lip glossing! The perfection that I assumed would wash over me had I had a big butt is seen in those photos and, for a split second, that desire comes back. However, in real life, the final product looks like a prop. Maybe the handful of BBLs I've seen weren't done "correctly," but instead of it looking like a peach, it was high and round, which is what I've always wanted, but it looked stiff and hard, which isn't what I wanted and, frankly, never saw growing up. I'm trying my best to explain this, but the idea of surgically enhancing my ass now felt like being gifted a floor-length red sequined dress. It's a gorgeous gift and would come in handy if attending a gala, or Barack Obama's inauguration party, but who is wearing a floor-length red sequined dress to Home Depot, or to the renter's office, or to buy gas? BBLs made booties look cartoonish to me, and I wasn't interested in letting go of one insecurity—of not having an ass—in exchange for having one that looked a little too out there. But even more than having seen a few in real life that weren't great, and not having the money to get the procedure done, was the small voice in the back of my head that found a microphone to ask a simple question: "For what?"

After years of wishing I had a bigger butt and looking at other women who I assumed had better figures and the lives to match, the idea of a BBL seemed excessive and risky. And then, one day, it hit me: nothing anyone had was ever going to make their life perfect, not even if they had the best ass on the block. My relentless pursuit of perfection had manifested in the behind I didn't possess. Yet it took some time for me to take stock of the women in my life who did have nice butts and for me to realize they weren't vacationing in Capri or casually buying high-end shoes and purses on a whim. The vending machine of life was also eating their dollars too. Their lives were as beautiful and as complicated as everyone else's life. Having bigger behinds didn't mean they didn't receive an unexpected bill or have to deal with some asshat who cut them off in traffic. Life was life-ing for everyone, whether you had a big booty, a little booty, or no booty at all. This all became clearer to me once BBLs became normalized and that same little voice that once asked: "For what?" quickly responded and said, "Nah, I'm good."

This isn't a chapter about body positivity as much as it is a chapter about body acceptance, and I've finally gotten to a place in my life where I'm (mostly) good with where I physically am. My former editor, Jerry, once succinctly said: "There's a billion-dollar industry based upon women's insecurities." His statement stuck with me because for more than half of my life, I felt less than because I didn't have a big booty and believed that if I had hit the lottery at the right time, I would've contributed my own dollars to that already thriving industry just to *feel* perfect. There's so much that we demand from women's bodies. They're to be healthy and pristine, to carry life, as well as taut, supple, and soft to entice. Our bosom is to be both a pillow for our children or partner when they need comfort, as well as a place where darting eyes land whenever we wear a V-neck, a crew neck, or even a turtleneck. There are days when I take a look at myself naked in the mirror and I think, "Not bad." I'll do a quick spin and notice a roll that has magically appeared, or I'll jiggle my arms and the inner tattoo on my left arm will flap. But then I'll look back at my bum and be okay. Over the years, with a slowing metabolism and the joys of the Popeyes' spicy chicken sandwich (real ones know the Wendy's spicy chicken was a pioneer), I've been able to get a little more cushion, not a lot but enough to look cheeky if the jeans I'm wearing are a little worn in or if I put on my favorite Old Navy athleisure leggings. If I'm wearing a pencil skirt that hugs me just right, I can give off the illusion that something's happening back there, and still, those moments feel good. The difference now is that I'm not salivating for them. I'm okay with where I'm at and with what I've got going on. When I'm at the gym, if the instructor tells us to grab a fifteen-pound weight for ten sumo squats, I grab a twenty-pound weight and do fifteen sumo squats. So, yes, there's still a teeny, tiny part of me that's attached to my big butt years, but the feeling is not as strong as before.

Wanting to look good, wanting to be perceived as beautiful, and hoping that beauty is recognized are all normal things. I also want to make it clear that if you've gotten any cosmetic surgery to enhance your body, you won't get any judgment from me. It's your body, your money, and your PTO. By all means. But there was a time in my life where I compared every other woman's body to mine and felt so . . . ugh! I'm thankful that, after everything, I can finally be good with where I am now.

My only regret is that I didn't get here sooner.

12

When the World Stood Still

"Think I should bring my sweater home? I keep it in the office whenever it gets cold," I asked my colleague Devin.

"I mean, you can," he said, stuffing his laptop charger into his backpack. "But you'll have to bring it back when this is all over."

"Point taken. I'll leave it."

It was March 13, 2020, and the CEO sent a company-wide email informing everyone, effective immediately, we'd be working from home until further notice. Over the past few months, a growing concern over a mysterious yet lethal virus had begun to dominate the news cycle, and small talk in and outside of the office.

Random Number One: *"Yo, what's the move for the night?"*

Random Number Two: *"Ion't even know for real. I'm waiting on LaQuelle to hit back. *texts heart face emoji to LaQuelle**

Random Number Three: *"Yo, y'all hear about that virus? That Corona shit?*

Random Number One: *"You already know Quelle ain't hittin' you back, bro. Y'all tryna hit up that one spot Uptown?"*

Random Number Two: *"Yo, how you sound? Me and LaQuelle talk."*

Random Number One: *"She stay leavin you on read! What's homeboy's name with the books and shit? LeVar Burton? That's you, wit yo reading reading rainbow ass."*

Random Number Two: *"Yeah, aigh't. Ion't know nothing about no Corona. People stay hyping shit up. It's the flu, dawg. I promise you."*

Random Number Three: *"People die from the flu though?"*

Random Number One: *"This clown bout to be dead before LaQuelle hit back, I know that!"*

As Devin and I continued our packing, the chatter in the office simmered. Soon, the sounds of metal drawers closing, rolling chairs dragging across the carpeted floor, and the gentle clap of MacBooks closing became the resounding chorus. It was about midday and under normal circumstances my team and I would be discussing our lunch plans and groaning over the redundancy from having ordered food from our usual haunts on Eighth or Ninth Avenue. Instead, we were packing up our bags to work from home . . . indefinitely.

"How long do you think we'll be gone?" I asked Devin.

"Six weeks maybe?"

"Really?" I said with wide eyes.

"I mean, I hope it doesn't take longer than that."

No one knew what to think or say. Devin's guess was about as good as anyone else's. It was a Friday, so leaving work early felt like the beginning of a four-day weekend, which helped mask the severity of everything. But once I left the building, I could feel a difference. It wasn't the normal noise pollution the city is known for, or the usual fast-walking New Yorker trapped behind a slow-walking tourist kind of annoyance. Instead, there was a thinly veiled unknowing that loomed, as if everyone was pretending things were fine, but we could all feel things weren't okay at all. I tightened my scarf, shoved my hands into my pockets, and continued my walk to the train unaware that the city that never sleeps would soon fall into a terrifying slumber.

. . .

Living through a catastrophic event isn't wavy, like, at all. You'd think being able to say: "I was there. I experienced the whole thing" would, in a weird way, give you some bragging rights, but I'd much rather read about the historic event than have to survive it. Unfortunately, global pandemics don't have good manners. A pandemic is like that one family member who always pops up unannounced. There was little time to mentally prepare for what was to come and how much would be lost. No one could quantify the grief we'd all experience as well as the collective boredom from not having anywhere to go or much to do. A caste system began to take shape. Grocery store clerks, postal workers, doctors, and nurses still had to commute to work, while I and many others had the privilege of having our groceries and food delivered while doing our jobs from the comfort and safety of our homes.

The sounds of ambulances going back and forth from emergency rooms became background noise for cities nationwide. Wearing or not wearing a mask was seen as a political statement. Hospitals bursting at the seams quickly ran out of beds for the stampede of new cases, while dying patients were deprived of the comfort of having family and friends by their side as they took their last breath. Hand sanitizer, Lysol, disinfecting wipes, and toilet paper, of all things, became some of the hottest commodities. Despite any reports indicating that we were using the bathroom more, people just didn't want their neighbors having more toilet paper than they did in the event prunes ousted Wheat Thins or potato chips as the new hit pandemic snack.

Trained medical professionals were being outdone by people with large social media followings who Googled "What would Dr. Sebi do?" or "ginger tea + covid." Sheltering in place was the best solve government officials could come up with, resulting in many victims being stuck inside with their abusers. Some folks had fine family lives, but cabin fever had them up against the ropes. For a lot of people, young ones especially, it was the lack of camaraderie with their friends and a social life that did them in. While the daily death toll climbed along with misinformation, our universal mental health was chipped away in large chunks like pieces of a melting iceberg crashing into a frigid ocean.

And this was just the first thirty days.

I was one of the fortunate ones. My job quickly made the transition from working in person to working remotely. Mommy's job closed down shortly after mine, but she was able to file for unemployment and, in essence, have six to eight weeks off for the first time in God knows how long. All of my friends were safe and for the ones who lost jobs, they freelanced before full-time work came along. I lived through the worst of the pandemic and yet I experienced its lightest touch. I had food. I had a job. I didn't miss rent. I even made frivolous purchases. One week it was a French press (despite my fully functioning coffee maker staring me right in the face) and the next it was the NARS Radiant Creamy Concealer in the shade Caramel (wasn't a fan of the applicator). Being able to buy things I didn't need when people could barely afford groceries was a privilege, but it was also an (expensive) coping mechanism. There was little joy to be had during the height of it all, so I literally *paid* for my happiness. With every tracking number that arrived in my inbox, I knew within two or three days something would show up at my doorstep and that brief high of receiving a package was how I'd be able to partially survive. I didn't drink. I didn't overeat. I didn't curl up into a ball. I didn't cry. I instead purchased an air fryer, a cast-iron skillet, a handheld mixer, and excessive amounts of Trader Joe's Mushroom & Company Multipurpose Umami Seasoning blend.

Eventually, the purchases slowed down and the "newness" of remote work lost its luster. As an adult, I either never have enough time or enough money. The pandemic, oddly enough, gave me more of both, and while I wasn't making the best financial decisions, I wanted to take inventory of my life and choices, which isn't so easy to do when you're always on the go. I didn't want to be one of those people who was too scared to ask myself *why*. I'm the common denominator in my life and I also think curiosity is such a formidable yet underused tool. Whether it be laziness, fear, or outright disinterest, I do not believe people question why they do the things they do or react in the way they react enough. I've always been someone who asked questions and with the pandemic and remote work, I finally had the chance to settle down and figure out the answer. Whether I was given two weeks or two years, I was committed to using this time in a way I felt was most productive. I guess that's a long-winded way to say I do not want to be ashy. When I say ashy, I don't just mean unmoisturized. I mean overall whack and corny! Curiosity of self can lead to self-awareness and self-discovery. Ashy people, in my book, could care less. *This is who I am, you either take it or leave it* is what members of the dry-skin community would say. The pandemic gave me the space to sit down, look at myself in the mirror, and examine who was staring back at me, and what I've gathered is I've been too hard on myself in some areas, while not going hard enough in others. My reflection is a combination of sorts, and these are just a few realizations of who I became when the world stood still.

1. I Found Confidence in Cooking

Who has time to roast a garlic and herb chicken when you have fifty-leven deadlines? Well, when you're in a global pandemic, you might have a few extra hours on hand to do just that. It took thirty-five years, but I finally learned how to cook and, to my surprise, I'm actually good at it! I started with simple meals and then worked my way to the tasty Jamaican dishes I grew up eating. Curry goat, curry chicken, curry Cheerios (It's jokes, y'all. No one is throwing curry seasoning on Honey Nut Cheerios.), oxtail, and the beloved Caribbean beverage sorrel were all recipes I tried and successfully made. And if I wasn't learning the cuisine of my mother and grandmother, I decided that I'd like to die by way of type 2 diabetes, so I also started baking. I made an apple pie and an apple cake. I baked bread and a pineapple upside-down cake. When my dear Betty White passed, I honored her life by baking an Oreo cheesecake. I made homemade doughnuts with white frosting and sprinkles as well as German chocolate cake all from scratch. I basically became the Black Betty Crocker, or Ebony Crocker, if you will. (Pay me in vanilla extract!) Don't get me wrong, there were definitely fails. After an hour in the oven at 350 degrees, my pound cake still wasn't cooked all the way through, and for whatever reason, my chocolate chip cookies always look like they were made in a meth lab on the set of *Breaking Bad*.

I'm a career-focused woman. I've worked diligently to get to where I am in life and cooking wasn't on my list of priorities. With countless food delivery services, I wasn't in a rush to get in the kitchen either. Yet after learning how to feed and bake for myself, I realized how much joy I could experience simply by making the crust of a pie or a delightfully boozy Jamaican black cake. I once thought this deep sense of pride could only come from a career accomplishment. I didn't know that knowing your way around the kitchen could be just as fulfilling. Cooking also made me feel like I had unlocked a new level of adulthood. Paying bills is one thing, doing laundry and cleaning up is another, but knowing how to cook made me feel like I had jumped and hit the gold coin box in *Super Mario Bros.* Now, I'm twice as big, twice as smart, and twice as powerful. And my baked mac and cheese is bomb.

2. *Leaning into Femininity Was Freeing and Gratifying*
   It's embarrassing to admit this, especially now since the Sephora and Ulta Beauty websites are literally my grief-counseling centers, but I never saw the value in investing in my beauty. I never *wanted* to lean into it, if I'm being honest. As a Black woman and a writer, I wanted to be taken "seriously" (whatever that means), and I didn't want men in my industry thinking all I cared about were my looks. It's an odd double standard if you think about it. When a man has a fancy car, a nice watch, and a big house, those materialistic items are proof he's a "real man," but if a woman enjoys makeup, having designer purses and shoes, and leans into her own softness, somehow, she's superficial or a gold digger.

   For so long I believed this, silently judging women who actually gave a damn about how they looked. "Real women" went to work, did responsible things with their money, took care of the house, bought groceries, and put gas in the car. Investing any of their coins in makeup, perfume, and fine clothing was frivolous and attention seeking. The women in my family didn't dress like hobos; hair and nails were standard upkeep, but full-on glam was not a thing. Femininity wasn't discouraged growing up, but it wasn't encouraged either. It was always *Yuh tek up yuh book from mawnin!?* Meaning, did you study? Did you do your homework? Did you double-check your math? There was a bigger emphasis on education than there was on my physical exterior, which can be par for the course as it pertains to Black girls, but the emotional development that comes with owning your beauty was something that was pushed to the side. Things changed for a spell as a teen. A midriff may have been exposed once or twice, and my backless champagne-colored prom dress was also a moment. I dabbled with black eyeliner missing my waterline completely, but that's beside the point. Once I stepped foot into my current industry, I defaulted to caring more about building my byline than my looks or freshening up my wardrobe.

If any woman put what I deemed to be too much time or effort into what she wore or how she looked, then she was clearly an empty vessel. "Real beauty" could only be found in one's intellect, and since all of this was informed by how I saw men interact and react to beautiful women, I kept this lie alive. Men weren't stopping women because they saw them reading Baldwin or Butler. They were approaching women because of how cute or sexy they looked, and if a man was going to approach me, my intelligence, or so I thought, would be the draw.

(Yes, I once truly believed this foolishness.)

But one of the best unforeseen side effects of the pandemic was not having to interact with men nearly as much. So, with them not being in the picture, I had a chance to look at beauty and fashion differently. Femininity is more than getting your eyebrows arched or putting on a cute skirt. It's about expressing your womanhood in the way *you* feel most comfortable. For too long I hid behind a prickly wall because I wanted everyone to know I was *not* the one to play games with, but deeper than that, I rarely met men who knew how to balance my brilliance and my beauty. Yes, I'm beautiful, but I read a lot of books, and yes, I read a lot of books, but also tell me I'm cute. Don't think because I'm one we can't acknowledge the other. So, if I had to decide which one of these attributes would take the back seat, I chose my looks. I used to think beauty and femininity were weaknesses, and I wasn't gonna let any man catch me slippin'.

Turns out, I was wrong, like *dead* wrong! Women who know how to wield a blending brush, line their lips, and put on a lash are actually wizards, like Dumbledore. The first time my cousin Tara filled my brows in and then cleaned them up with concealer I was blown away. I looked ten times better and I felt twenty times more confident. I liked that feeling and wanted more of it. I also enjoyed the softness that came over me. Gone was the prickly outer shell and in its place a more open, welcoming woman. Soon after, I became obsessed with YouTube makeup tutorials, trying to emulate their technique in hopes to recreate a look for myself. What initially jumped out at me was the power. I didn't realize this strength comes with knowing how to adorn yourself, or how much practice and skill it requires. I saw the confidence and ease women exuded when they felt good about themselves. These women looked like they were comfortable in their skin; it wasn't too loose or too tight, and that confidence is something I longed for. If ever I completed a look and it *actually* came out correct, it was an instant confidence booster that called for a celebratory twerk in the mirror. This realization eventually helped me see that my feminine side wasn't my weaker side. It was actually a portal through which I could gain more insight and strength.

3. *I've Inched Closer to Forgiveness*

Forgiveness is still *very* difficult for me, but over the pandemic I got a little closer to it by way of acceptance. I still obsess over why things happen the way they do. With Stephen, I wanted him to like me, and it was disappointing when he didn't. With Kimberly, her "absolute loyalty" jab would echo in my head for years, shaping me in ways that spawned a lot of self-doubt. The trauma from Redacted, however, shook me and my foundation, resulting in relentless questioning. Wanting to get to the truth is logical and understandable, but I realized asking questions and not finding the answers only fed the trauma and watered my frustration and anger. It also kept me in a continuous cycle of re-victimizing myself. I was doing the work for the people who hurt me!

But then it hit me: Even if I did receive the answers to questions from those who had caused me pain, that wouldn't change anything. In fact, it would probably piss me off more, so I finally concluded I can either get lost in the past or accept that it happened and try to move on. And that's what I did. I put one leg in front of the other and started to move on. I don't want to be some old lady still singing about an old hurt that happened decades earlier. I don't want my past to have any control over my present and co-opt any space or time in my future. Holding on to hurt feels like an emotional clog, and acceptance is the only "plumbing" that seems to work. My hope is that once I clear this drain, I can make room within myself to feel other emotions, like contentment, peace, and maybe even joy.

Anger and pain take up a lot of emotional and mental square footage. They change your perspective and color how you view things. They make you insecure and also ensure that you continue to be a victim. There are instances in life where you've undoubtedly been made to be the victim, but in my tireless obsession over the past, I *remained* the victim for a lot longer than I needed to. It was corrosive because I stayed in a space in which I was the one re-cutting and re-breaking my own heart. Who wants that?

I want to view things as objectively as possible without my negative past experiences clouding the present, which requires a lot of work but is doable. Anger is also super-duper heavy and, so far, acceptance feels lighter. I haven't fully let everything go; I still have a rehearsed script saved in notes if I run into Redacted's ass. Forgiveness may still not be my jam, but for me acceptance is a big first step.

4. *My Return to Sender Game Is . . . Better*
Years ago I went to my friend Tiffany's house. We made plans to see the latest *Fast and Furious* movie, and before we left, Tiff texted a mutual friend of ours to see what she was doing and if she wanted to hang out afterward. The friend responded, "I'm not in charge of everyone's social life!" Tiff read the text, grimaced, and said aloud, "I don't know what that's all about, but I know that ain't for me."

Tiffany removed herself from the snappy response and we happily went about our day. That moment stuck with me because this kind of emotional awareness isn't something

I've always had. Any backlash or anger that I may have received felt like it was something I deserved. I would take those instances so personally and beat myself up for upsetting the other person, not considering all the context and variables. As I've gotten older, I recognize misdirected anger is *such* a thing. It can be ferocious, alarming, and catch you off guard, to say the least. It's easier to identify when you're on the outside looking in, but when you're the victim of it, it becomes harder to pinpoint. Marveling at how easily Tiffany was able to let that comment roll off her back, I could've saved myself a lot of emotional and mental anguish if I had adopted that kind of thinking earlier.

Our mutual friend tried to throw her junk in Tiffany's mailbox, but it was swiftly returned to sender and now I'm beginning to do the same. When things go left, I examine myself and what I've brought to the situation. Was I rude? Insensitive? Inconsiderate? Hurtful? If so, then that mail *does* belong in my mailbox, and I'll deal with it. Other than that, I won't allow anyone else's ish and misdirected *anything* stick to me and become my problem. You can take up all that unresolved mess with your out-of-network therapist, sis.

5. *Everything Takes Time*

Earlier in this book, I complained about not having a big butt. Growing up in a household where everyone had curves except me was tough. One day, when I was about fourteen my aunt Lavern told me if I wanted a butt, all I had to do was squats. The simple strength exercise would be the answer to all my body insecurities. All I had to do was stand up straight, plant my feet hip distance apart, lower my body, and then squeeze my bum on the way back up. If I did this a hundred times a day consistently for a year, I'd see a notable difference in my backside.

Did I start doing squats though? Of course not.

Well, why didn't you?

For the same reason a lot of people don't immediately start doing what's good for them when they're told. When the world opened back up, I decided to get a gym membership, and I'm happy to say, I work out about two or three times a week. And now, as forty flirts with me from across the room, I'm finally beginning to get the butt I've always wanted, one I could've had years ago had I done what Auntie suggested.

So, what's the point?

The point is, I've learned that the distance between knowing what to do and actually doing it isn't as narrow a distance as I once assumed. Oftentimes, there's more life you've got to live before hearing something once and then putting it into practice. That time in between can be growing pains, building blocks, character development, laziness, hard-headedness, time spent in witness protection, whatever. For some people it can take a few months, for others their entire life. I'm a slow learner, so it takes me years to actually do something I know is good for me, which isn't a flex at all. Now, I'm all about the lunges, donkey kicks, and goblet squats. I wish I had started this when Auntie told me to, not because I would've had a fatty right now, but maybe it would've clicked that if you do the right thing sooner you benefit from it sooner as well.

And I don't care what anyone says, burpees are a form of white supremacy. I'll die on this hill.

. . .

I'm sure if I noodled on this a bit more, I could think of three or four more areas of growth that happened for me over the pandemic, but these five are the ones that stick out the most. I don't know if I would've had the time to grow into this current space had it not been for the pandemic, and even with the time it provided, I know now more than ever how challenging it is to be your best and do your best. It can feel like a full-time job, and I get why some people give up. Holding yourself accountable while giving yourself grace is a juggling act if ever I've seen one. Advocating for yourself while trying to sympathize or empathize with the other person requires you to play emotional double Dutch. Knowing the difference between being given constructive criticism and someone projecting or trying to manipulate you is an Olympic sport. Learning to cut your losses often requires having taken one too many losses in the past. Gaining the confidence to set a boundary is one thing, but learning to be okay with the other person's irritation or anger about your boundary is a whole different ball game. And get this: the real chamomile, Earl Grey, peppermint, ginger, black tea is realizing that even when you go to therapy, and you do the work, and you use your tools, *and* you're brave enough to be vulnerable, sometimes doing it the "healthy" way does not merit you a new cookie. The studio audience doesn't *always* start clapping and no one comes out and brings you a new Cuisinart Food Processor. The emotional maturity one has to have on a daily basis just to grow even the teeniest, tiniest amount is breathtaking and time-consuming. I guess what I'm getting at is that living is hard, and it's even harder when you want to be your best, especially during a global pandemic.

But what other choice do I really have?

Do I resign to giving up on myself? Do I not even allow myself to be curious about the newer, shinier, funnier, caring-er version of Shenequa? Don't we all have to try? Because if there's one thing this pandemic has hammered home for me, it's that we're all going to die one day. One day it'll be curtains for all of us, and you can either go to your grave empty, having given this life and your loved ones your best, or you can die full, bloated with unreleased care, potential, love, and promise. The latter, to me, sounds terrifying.

As I'm writing this, Devin, myself, and the rest of my colleagues still haven't made our way back to the office and, honestly, we don't know if we'll ever have to. The world is different now. We don't have to go back to the old work model to be successful, and to keep it real with you, I don't want to go back to the old version of Shenequa. Don't get me wrong; she worked and was hella cute. Shenequa of yesteryear got me to this point safely and with tremendous grace and humor and that's all anyone can really ask for. But the new Shenequa—who's leaning into her softer side, knows her way around the kitchen, and understands the difference between loose setting powders and finishing powders—is here and ready to take up space. This Shenequa is taller, smarter, and better, and maybe her flaws are taller too, who knows? As it stands *right* now, the new Shenequa is sipping on a honey hazelnut iced latte (with oat milk) taking it one step at a time and confident she'll be aight when push and its homie shove pull up, like they're known to do. This Shenequa is the mood and the moment, and I cannot wait to see how far she takes me.

BIG UPS AND SHOUT-OUTS

This is bananas! I've written a book. What is life right now? Okay, to begin, I want to send a special shout-out to my record label, Death Row Records. Y'all saw the vison early.

Kidding.

I want to begin by thanking my agent, Kathy, and the entire team at Jane Rotrosen Agency. I have no idea how my story made its way to you, but I'm so thankful it did and even more grateful you believed I could write a book. A super big shout-out to Beacon Press and an even bigger shout-out to the avengers of editing who assembled to help make these essays the best they can be. Big ups to Tracy Garraud for being the earliest set of eyes on some of these chapters. (Fun fact: I was going to self-publish a collection of stories back in 2018 and enlisted Tracy to edit, but then God was like: "Baby girl, sit down. I've got something better in mind.") Shout out to Fernanda Martinez for helping me get my proposal in shape, Maya Fernandez for letting me write wildly and freely and understanding the power of Black girlness, and last but most certainly not least, the Ironman of them all, Jenn Baker. Jenn came through with her red pen and helped me get to work! Thank you, Jenn. Your expertise coupled with your gentle approach felt like a thousand spring days.

Thank you to my lawyer for your thorough, legal eye. Even though you went to Howard, I think I'll keep you. (Don't I owe you a drink?) Thank you to Datwon Thomas and Christine Imarenezor for always being a listening ear. A lot happened while I was writing this book and I don't think either of you realize how valued you both made me feel while I was swimming through oceans of worthlessness. Thank you.

Big ups to Damon Young. Getting an agent and writing a proposal was not on my 2020 Bingo card, but it happened, and I had no idea what I was doing. Through countless G-Chats and convos on the phone, Damon, you helped me put my proposal together, which, if we're being honest, is half the battle. Thank you for all your help and guidance.

Thank you, David Dennis Jr. A few weeks after I got my book deal, I took a social media break because life was kicking my ass. You were the only one who noticed and reached out. From there, a friendship blossomed, and despite your busy schedule and your own writing, you read my chapters, offered valid critiques, and reminded me that the finish line was a lot closer than what it felt like at the time. Thank you, shuga. You deserve all the cinnamon rolls and none of the calories.

I also want to shout-out a few Black writers I've looked up to and admired since forever: Demetria Lucas, Aliya King, and Clover Hope. These three women have always done the work and then quietly gone about their business, not needing or looking for fanfare or praise. Thank you for carving out careers and allowing little Black girls like me to see how it can be done.

Shout-out to Shanita Hubbard, Justin Tinsley, and Sylvia Obel for also giving me their honest feedback on some of my early chapters. Writers and authors know how demanding this craft is and what it's like, and we need each other to survive. I randomly reached out, dropped five thousand words on y'all like you all didn't have full-time jobs, kids, and lives of your own, and asked for your help, and because y'all are so dope, you all looked out and actually helped me. I never forget when people come through for me. Thank you. Truly.

To everyone who's ever called Oceania Street home, thank you so much (that includes you too, Dally): Greg, Auntie Floret, Auntie Alma, Auntie Marie, to my "dad" Auntie Lavern, I think even Uncle Bunny stayed at the house for a bit, no? Tisha, Ian, Tara, Tameka, Kim (I love you) Diamond, and the biggest boss of them all, Minna Louise Williams.

To the prettiest girl in the world, Mommy. It was your idea that I become a writer. I don't think you thought I was going to listen to you, but turns out, you were right! Thank you for giving me the space to chase this dream and, more importantly, never telling me to give up during the early years when there was no proof any of this would turn out like it has. I love you, babes!

Thank you to God for carrying me through and protecting me even from my own foolishness.

I want to send a super big shout-out to my therapist. There was a lot of hurt, confusion, and loneliness I experienced as I penned these chapters, and I'd often email or call asking if you had additional availability outside of our weekly sessions. On the days you could, you helped me clean up my own emotional mess and regain my bearings. Thank you so very much.

Shout-out to you, the reader. You literally do not have to read my book and you did. Thank you!

And to any girl, especially Black girls, who loves reading books and loves writing stories but is a little left of center and isn't quite comfortable in her skin just yet. It's all good. I was there. Keep reading, keep writing, and I promise, you'll figure it out in your own way and in your own time. You got this, baby girl. I promise.

NOTES

ONE: BLACK GIRL MATH

1. Little-T and One Track Mike (Timothy Sullivan and Michael Flannery), "Shaniqua (Don't Live Here No More)," Lava/Atlantic Records, 2001.
2. Randee Dawn, "Raven-Symone Calls Name Discrimination Comments 'Poor Taste,'" Today.com, October 12, 2015, https://www.today .com/popculture/raven-symone-calls-name-discrimination-comments -poor-taste-t49441.
3. Ari Shapiro, "Dr Marijuana Pepsi Won't Change Her Name 'To Make Other People Happy,'" NPR, June 22, 2019, https://www .npr.org/2019/06/21/734839666/dr-marijuana-pepsi-wont-change -her-name-to-make-other-people-happy.

TWO: KIMBERLY

1. Jane Doe, text message to author, February 2014.

THREE: REDACTED

1. Text message correspondence to author, April 16, 2020.
2. John Doe e-mail message to author, June 1, 2020.
3. Stephanie Hargrove, MA, "Intimate Partner Violence in the Black Community," National Center on Violence Against Women in the Black Community, October 2018, https://ujimacommunity.org/ wp-content/uploads/2018/12/Intimate-Partner-Violence-IPV-v9.4.pdf.
4. Card to author, October 2019.

FOUR: A SEPTEMBER KISS

1. Shenequa Golding, email to subject, December 3, 2017.

FIVE: TWO SUGARS WITH HAZELNUT CREAM

1. David A. Frederick et al., "Differences in Orgasm Frequency Among Gay, Lesbian, Bisexual, and Heterosexual Men and Women in a U.S. National Sample," *Archives of Sexual Behavior* 47 (2018): 273–88, https://link.springer.com/article/10.1007/s10508-017-0939-z.
2. *George Michael: Freedom Uncut*, dir. David Austin and George Michael, Sony Music Entertainment, 2017, https://www.georgemichael freedomuncut.com.

SEVEN: JAGGED LITTLE PILL

1. "Oprah and Iyanla Vanzant's Misunderstanding," *The Oprah Winfrey Show*, February 16, 2011, https://www.oprah.com/own-oprahshow/oprah-and-iyanla-vanzants-misunderstanding-video.
2. "The Different Types of Anger," Better Help, February 18, 2023, https://www.betterhelp.com/advice/anger/are-there-different-levels-of-anger.
3. Shenequa Golding, email to Jane Doe, October 2022.
4. Jane Doe, email to author, October 2022.

TEN: LOWERED EXPECTATIONS

1. "Boyz 'R Us," *Martin*, season 1, episode 4, written by Martin Lawrence, John Bowman, and Carew Tapper, dir. Tony Singletary, aired September 17, 1992, on Fox.

ELEVEN: BBL

1. "Aesthetic Plastic Surgery National Databank Statistics," Aesthetic Society, 2020, https://cdn.theaestheticsociety.org/media/statistics/aestheticplasticsurgerynationaldatabank-2020stats.pdf.
2. Abby Ellen, "Brazilian Butt Lifts Surge, Despite Risks," *New York Times*, August 19, 2021, updated October 27, 2021, https://www.ny times.com/2021/08/19/style/brazillian-butt-lift-bbl-how-much-risks.